Publication Number 7 in the ''On Target''
Series of outdoor sports publications
from Glenn Helgeland's
TARGET COMMUNICATIONS

1st Edition
Printings: 1/89; 2nd, 8/89
2nd Edition
Printings: 1st, 7/90; 2nd,
5/91; 3rd, 9/92; 4th, 10/93;
5th, 6/95

On Target for

TUNING YOUR BROADHEADS

and your entire
HUNTING BOW SYSTEM

*(including Fast Flight cable system
and carbon arrows)*

by Larry Wise

with Sherwood Schoch
and Glenn Helgeland

Special Technical Assistance
from Norb Mullaney

Library of Congress Number: 89-50077

TARGET COMMUNICATIONS CORPORATION
7626 W. Donges Bay Rd.
Mequon, WI 53092

ISBN: 0-913305-08-1

AUTHOR'S ACKNOWLEDGEMENTS

Many special people have given their time, ideas and advice throughout the creation of this book. They deserve more recognition than these few sentences could possibly give.

They are:

Norb Mullaney, who is a continual source of correct and valuable information on the scientific principles and testing related to archery. The information and corrections he provided for this book are extremely vital to its completeness. I'm privileged to have him as a friend, and his help is most appreciated.

Sherwood Schoch, who has taken time from a very busy schedule to contribute valuable thoughts and information in the form of a chapter to this book. His advice and friendship always have high value.

Glenn Helgeland, who continues to support my effort at writing with great editing skills. He has taken my rather plain and mathematical style and made it more readable. His publishing efforts will enable me to extend my education career to a worldwide group of interested and information-hungry bowhunters.

Jon Wert, who, with his pen and pencil, has added clarity and beauty to this book by doing the illustrations that photography couldn't. His talent is greatly appreciated.

Ginny Haubert, who, once again, has given me lessons in paragraph structure and organization. Her time and talent have made this book a good effort in communication.

Dennis Spancake, who did a fine job on the photos for this book.

Diana, Jennifer and **Todd,** who tolerated my hectic schedule while I was writing this book.

To all of these special people, I extend a sincere "thanks".

Dedication

This book is dedicated to Ruth Hampton. We pray that our memories of her will move us to do good things.

Contents

Larry Wise: Biographical Sketch

Born in a farming area of Pennyslvania, Larry was an instant candidate for hunting of any kind. When his father bought two archery sets in 1958, both began a lifelong pursuit of the whitetail deer with bows and arrows.

Bowhunting led to tournament archery, whereupon Larry collected his share of trophies in the barebow division. College and an early career in public education interrupted tournament archery, but the bowhunting continued.

Larry bought his first compound bow in 1976 and the archery bug once again bit strong. Since then, he has taken 15 deer with the bow and established himself as one of the top professional archers in the world. Besides winning numerous state championships, he has won 10 nationally recognized tournaments, including the Big Sky Open, the Atlantic City Classic, the 1987 Coors Silver Dollar Open and the Milwaukee Sentinel Sport Show.

Larry and his partners (Jack Cramer in 1979, 80 and 81, Ron Waller in 1985 and 87) have won five World Team Championships. Larry and Dean Pridgen teamed in 1988 to win the NFAA Indoor team title and finish second in the NFAA Outdoor team event. Larry and his partners have won more than $30,000 in these events alone.

His most impressive statistic is winning the 1986-87 IFAA World Professional Field Archery Championship in Blair Atholl, Scotland.

One of the industry's brightest stars, Larry broadened himself by learning and applying a great deal of technical information about the compound bow. That same valuable information is shared with all readers in this easy-to-follow book.

Larry, his wife Diana, daughter Jennifer, and son Todd live in rural Juniata County, Pennsylvania.

Chapter 1

The Broadhead Tuning Test

Take the following test. The results may be very interesting and will tell you your strong and weak points of broadhead tuning.

TRUE OR FALSE

T/F

_____ 1. A broadhead-equipped arrow should hit the target at the same place as a field point-equipped arrow.

_____ 2. The blades of a three-blade broadhead must be aligned with the three fletches of the arrow.

_____ 3. The blades of a four-blade broadhead must be aligned with the four fletches of the arrow.

_____ 4. Shooting with fingers on the string or shooting with a release aid generally will require about the same draw length.

_____ 5. Shooting an arrow uphill requires that you aim slightly high.

_____ **6.** Shooting an arrow downhill requires that you aim slightly low.

_____ **7.** The arrow rest tension should not be changed when switching from field points to broadheads.

_____ **8.** The nocking point should not be changed when switching from field points to broadheads.

_____ **9.** A point of impact of your arrows should not change when a filled bow quiver is installed on the bow.

_____ **10.** The compound bow must be shot from the "middle of the valley" to obtain the best groups.

_____ **11.** When a light arrow and a heavy arrow are shot from the same bow, the lighter arrow will be faster and have more penetration.

_____ **12.** A punch-point broadhead will have more penetration than a broadhead which has a cutting edge for a point.

_____ **13.** Feather fletching will stabilize a broadhead quicker than vanes of equal size.

_____ **14.** Changing to a different style but the same weight broadhead should not require any retuning.

_____ **15.** The draw weight of your compound bow should not be changed when switching from field points to broadheads.

The answers:

1. False	6. True	11. False
2. False	7. False	12. False
3. False	8. False	13. True
4. False	9. False	14. False
5. False	10. True	15. False

How did you do? 14-15 correct — Master Tuner
10-13 correct — Expert Tuner
5-9 correct — Novice Tuner
0-4 correct — Non-Tuner

The answers to these and many other questions are discussed in this book. Read on.

Common Vocabulary Terms for Bow Tuning

Before you can use this book to your best advantage, you must understand the terminology of the subject. By reading over these important definitions now you can insure a good understanding of the many aspects of tuning a bow. **Don't skip this section!!!**

Arrow Length: The length of shaft as measured from the inset of the nock to the end of the shaft, not including the point.

Bare Shaft Testing: The use of non-fletched arrows at close range for adjusting nocking point and plunger stiffness.

Blade: The cutting edge part of the hunting arrow point which protrudes beyond the sides of the arrow shaft.

Bow Efficiency: The percent of stored energy of a bow which is transferred to the arrow at the time of release.

Broadhead: The entire assembly of parts used for a hunting arrow point.

Bow Sight: A device which can be attached to the handle riser above the arrow rest to hold one or more sight pins.

Brace Height: The perpendicular distance between the bowstring and the grip of the handle riser.

Cable Extension: The length of cable which wraps around the eccentric wheel and is attached to the bowstring.

Cable Saver: A small plastic device which can be placed on the cables of a compound bow, between the cables and the cable guard extension rod, so the rod does not wear through the plastic covering of the cables and so the cables cause less noise.

Centershot: The left/right placement of the arrow rest above the center of the grip of the handle riser.

Cushion Plunger: A spring-loaded device mounted through the handle riser against which the side of the arrow rests.

Draw Length Adjustment Brackets: A pylon mounted near the upper and lower ends of the handle riser used to adjust draw length on four-wheel compound bows.

Draw Length: The distance at full draw from the nocking point to the grip is the "true draw length", and the distance at full draw from the nocking point to the side of the bow farthest from the archer is "traditional draw length".

Dynamic Deflection: The amount of limb bend at full draw.

Dynamic Efficiency: See Bow Efficiency.

Eccentric Cam: A non-round wheel usually placed at the ends of the limbs and used to cause a decrease in the amount of weight held on the bowstring when the bow is at full draw.

Eccentric Wheel: A round wheel usually placed at the ends of the limbs and used to cause a decrease in the amount of weight held on the bowstring when the bow is at full draw.

Ferrule: The metal barrel portion of the broadhead onto which the blades, point and locking collars are mounted.

Filament Reinforced Limbs: Compound bow limbs constructed of modern plastic materials and reinforced with filaments which run the entire length of the limb.

Finger Release: The use of one's fingers and a finger protection device such as a tab placed directly on the bowstring for the purpose of drawing and releasing.

Force-Draw Curve: The graph created by plotting draw weight against draw length for a bow as it is drawn to full draw.

Four-Wheel Compound: A compound bow with an eccentric wheel attached to each limb tip and an idler wheel attached near the middle of each limb with cables connecting each wheel to the opposite idler and a draw length pylon on the opposite end of the handle riser.

Handle Riser: The wood or metal handle section to which the bow limbs are attached.

Helical Fletching: The method of placing fletches onto the arrow shaft in a spiral curve around the shaft.

Let-Off: The amount of weight reduction from peak weight to valley weight or holding weight.

Line Of Maximum Leverage: A straight line drawn from the axle of an eccentric wheel or cam through the center of the wheel or cam to the opposite side.

Modules: A semi-circular or semi-cam-shaped piece of plastic or metal that can be removed from the eccentric and replaced by a slightly larger or smaller piece to change the draw length of the compound bow.

Multiple Draw Eccentric: An eccentric wheel or cam with two or more slots into which the cable can be placed in order to generate different draw lengths.

Nocking Point: The location on the string at which the nock of the arrow is positioned for drawing and releasing.

Over-Draw Rest: An arrow rest placed between the handle riser and the bowstring, enabling the archer to use a shorter than normal arrow.

Paper Test: The use of a newspaper and picture frame for the purpose of recording the movements of the point end and nock end of an arrow after it leaves the bow.

Peak Weight: The highest weight level achieved during the draw stroke of a bow.

Peep Sight: A small metal or plastic disk containing a hole and placed in the bowstring above the nock of the arrow and used as a rear sight.

Powder Test: The use of white spray powder on the fletched end of an arrow to determine contact between fletching and arrow rest.

Reflex Limb: The limb design which uses limb tips that bend away from the shooter such as those found on the recurve bow.

Release Aid: A hand-held mechanical device which is attached to the bowstring and used to draw and release the string.

Return Cable: The length of cable which attaches an eccentric wheel to the axle of the opposite wheel.

Rocker: The plastic half-round pivot placed between the bow limb and the handle riser.

Side Plate: Part of the arrow rest used in place of a cushion plunger to support the side of the arrow.

Shoot-Around Rest: An arrow rest which requires the bottom-most fletch of the arrow to pass to the outside of the support arm of the rest.

Shoot-Through Rest: An arrow rest which requires the botttom-most fletch of the arrow to pass between the support arm of the rest and the handle riser.

Spine: The amount of bend in an arrow shaft caused by a two-pound weight placed in the center of the shaft.

Stacking: The greater rate of draw weight increase experienced when a longbow or recurve bow is drawn past its intended draw length.

Static Deflection: The amount of limb bend before the bow is drawn. Pre-bend is sometimes used to refer to static deflection.

Stored Energy: The amount of energy contained in the limbs when the bow is at full draw.

Tiller: The perpendicular distance from the string to the point where the limb meets the handle riser.

Two-Wheel Compound: A compound bow having one wheel on each limb tip and a cable system connecting each wheel with the axle of the opposite wheel.

Valley: The point of lowest holding weight on the string reached near full draw on a compound bow.

Vented Blade: The broadhead blade that has part of its center area removed so the surface area of the blade is decreased and less air resistance results.

Wall: The location at which rapid weight increase on the string begins when drawing a compound bow beyond the valley.

Weight Adjustment Bolt: The bolt placed through the butt end of the limb which attaches the limb to the handle riser and controls the peak weight of the limb system.

Wood Core Limbs: A bow limb constructed of two layers of fiberglass veneer between which a layer of wood laminations is placed.

Yoke Button: The small, round plastic wheel used in the cable system of the compound bow which divides the return cable load into two parts and distributes that load to both sides of the axle. It may also be used to shorten or lengthen the cable to adjust draw length.

• *Fig. 1. As you reach full draw, the deer hesitates with its boilerroom behind a tree. You wait. Success now depends on patience and one shot . . . and how well you have prepared for it.*

Introduction To Tuning Broadheads

It's 6:45 a.m. Bow season opened two weeks ago, and you haven't been able to position yourself for a good shot on any of the three bucks you saw during preseason scouting. The stand location you are using this morning — one of several you have prepared, so you'll always have a fresh stand no matter what the wind, food and cover conditions — is 20 yards west of the location you used a few days ago and is downwind of heavy cover which has a frequently used trail that passes a scrape some 50 yards to the north. The changing air movement this morning may cause some problems, but your clothes are clean, and you showered when you got up this morning. Maybe luck will be with you.

Then, on your right, movement catches your eye. Two does approach, stop and glance back, and then pass on. Several minutes go by before movement comes from 50 yards further to the right and back in the brush along the trail. It's a large deer. Maybe it will be one of the three bucks you saw before season.

Slowly the deer works its way toward you. You spot antlers. How about that! It is one of the bucks you saw earlier, the eight-pointer. If it continues in this direction, you may get one chance for a shot when it crosses an open area about 22 yards upwind. As you mentally run through your draw and aim procedure and watch the animals movements, it moves closer to the open area but stops behind a large bush.

This is it. You must draw now and be ready for the one shot you're going to get at this buck.

Your mouth is full of cotton as the deer takes several more steps into the open area. You aim and . . . . .

What happens now depends on the time and effort you put in tuning your bow and your broadheads. It doesn't have to take a lot of time, but you must invest enough time in doing the right things. That's where this book comes into the picture. The methods and techniques in this book can help you get better results in less time than you've been needing previously. The time you save tuning your bowhunting setup can be put to use in preseason scouting and extra practice. When all of these skills are blended in the right proportions, the result will be success in the field.

Do your homework and make that first shot count.

The need to maintain high standards in all aspects of bowhunting still remains — and always will remain — even though today's technology has increased the effective range of the bow and arrow for most bowhunters. The modern archer must be aware of the adjustments he or she needs to make on today's bows just as the American Indian knew all of his equipment. You must spend time working on arrows and broadheads to insure that they launch and fly right. Shooting form must be developed so you can take advantage of your bow's capabilities, have confidence in your equipment and your form and concentrate on the right things at the moment of truth. Without careful and thorough preparation in all aspects of your bowhunting efforts, you have much less chance to be successful.

Maintaining high hunting standards requires many things, and one of them is equipment knowledge. That's the reason for this book. If we don't spend time and effort with our hunting equipment and get it set up and tuned right, we will be less than successful; we will be anti-successful. Anti-success means that we would work against our tradition and our heritage, because poorly tuned — and thus poorly performing — equipment gives an inaccurate impression of the effectiveness of the hunting bow and arrow.

Good tuning means that you **consistently** can hit the broadhead target in your yard, set your sight pins and be positive that the shot you make from your hunting stand — or wherever you are — will go where it is aimed. Assuming, of course, that your shooting form doesn't break down and your concentration remains high and on the factors it should remain on — aiming properly and shooting when you should shoot.

Now and then, naturally, there will be an unseen twig which reaches out and kicks your arrow off track, but that comes with the territory. Sometimes, too, the animal will move unexpectedly, or a vagrant breeze will blow your scent to the animal and ruin everything, but those are the chances you take. That's also why it is called hunting instead of shooting.

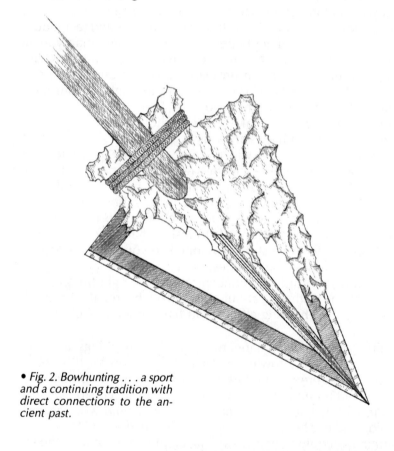

• Fig. 2. Bowhunting . . . a sport and a continuing tradition with direct connections to the ancient past.

Broadhead Tuning Test

Chapter 2

The Force-Draw Curve

With little effort, today's archer can find a bow test report in many archery magazines. After describing the parts of the individual bow being tested, the article will show the graph of the bow's force-draw curve. The purpose of this inclusion is to give you a picture of the work being done when the bow is drawn to the full-draw position.

The force-draw curve tells you about several important features of the bow being used. The most obvious of these is the actual draw weight that the archer would be feeling on the string of the bow at each position throughout the draw cycle. Another aspect that can be read from the force-draw curve is the stored energy of the bow. The location of the valley, in the case of the compound bow, is the third characteristic shown in the force-draw curve.

If you know the basics of the force-draw curve, then you will be better able to prepare the bow for hunting.

The Force-Draw Curve of the Longbow

By 1957, bowhunting was becoming very popular in central Pennsylvania where I was growing up. I was impressed by neighbors on either side of me; each had hunting bows and hunted deer in October. Charlie, our neighbor to the west, had a longbow and cedar shafts with broadheads and talked of the deer he would see on his hunting trips.

As a ten-year-old, I was greatly influenced and had to have a bow. Dad bought me a straight fiberglass Phantom bow which could be shot from left or right side. My archery career was off and running.

I soon discovered that shooting a straight bow was a little more work than I had bargained for. The further I drew the bow, the more force was needed. It didn't take long to learn that this continuous increase of the weight was not going to be easy to live with. However, I kept working at it and soon could hit the cardboard-filled Tide box that was my target.

The force-draw curve of the long or straight bow shows how the draw weight increases as the bow is drawn. The following graph (Fig. 3) is found in an article by C. N. Hickman for the *Franklin Institute Journal,* October, 1929.

The lemonwood bow used in Hickman's experiments reached a draw weight of 32 pounds of force at 28 inches draw length. Of course, if the archer continued to draw the bow, the weight continued to increase in an almost straight-line fashion. Looking carefully, you can detect a slight curve in the force-draw curve of the longbow.

GRAPH A.

• *Fig. 3. The draw weight of the longbow continues to increase as the bowstring is drawn. At the end of the draw stroke, the weight increases at a faster rate.*

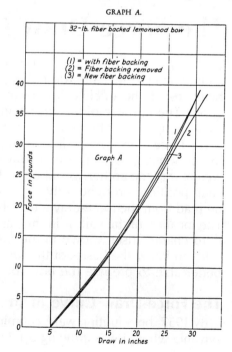

Force-Draw Curve

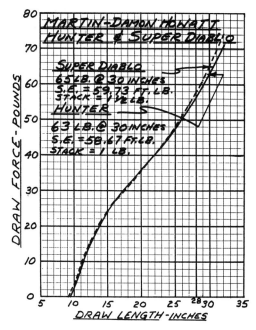

The graph shows:

Title: MARTIN-DAMON HOWATT HUNTER & SUPER DIABLO

SUPER DIABLO
65 LB. @ 30 INCHES
S.E. = 59.73 FT. LB.
STACK = 1½ LB.

HUNTER
63 LB. @ 30 INCHES
S.E. = 58.67 FT. LB.
STACK = 1 LB.

Y-axis: DRAW FORCE - POUNDS (0 to 80)
X-axis: DRAW LENGTH - INCHES (5 to 35)

NFM
4-25-88

• Fig. 4. The force-draw curve of the recurve bow is less steep near full draw. The recurve bow should feel smoother than the longbow.

The Force-Draw Curve Of The Recurve Bow

While the longbow shows a draw weight that increases at a greater and greater rate, the recurve bow does not. The force-draw curve of the recurve bow increases greatly during the first part of the draw cycle, but as the reflexed tips begin to bend the increase in weight lessens its rate. The recurve does not "stack" as much as the longbow from the middle to the end of the draw cycle and, therefore, feels smoother to draw.

The curve in Figure 4 is from the October, 1988, *Archery World* magazine bow report by Norb Mullaney. It demonstrates that by building the right recurve limbs, the increase in weight at the beginning of the draw cycle can be greater for the recurve than the longbow. This effect can be used to cause the limbs of the recurve to store more energy than the longbow. The lower rate of increase in weight for the recurve limb during the second half of the draw can cause the recurve bow to have less holding weight at full draw than the longbow, but the recurve can still have more stored energy.

The overall result will be an increase in the area under the force-draw curve for the recurve bow as compared to the longbow. This usually means that the arrow will get more energy and more speed from the recurve bow when compared to a longbow of equal weight.

The Force-Draw Curve Of The Compound Bow

The compound bow takes even more advantage of the fast increase in draw weight during the first half of the draw cycle. By using short, stiff limbs and an eccentric wheel system, the compound bow generates a fast increase in draw weight on the bowstring and then transfers the increasing weight to the power cable (inner) side of the eccentric wheel (see Figs. 5 & 6). After the transfer, the bowstring will experience a decrease in draw weight. The overall effect will be a substantial increase in the area under the force-draw curve. This means that the bow system has stored more energy, and more energy in the system **usually** but not always means more speed for the arrow.

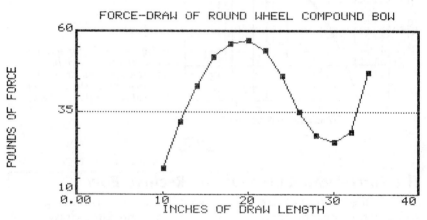

• *Fig. 5. The round wheels of a compound bow cause the weight to increase rapidly to peak weight, then decrease into the valley. Beyond the valley, the weight begins to increase rapidly.*

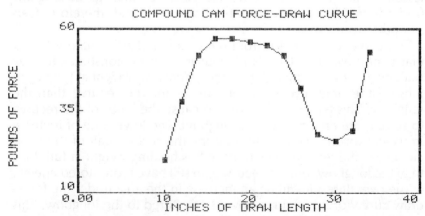

• *Fig. 6. The cam-shaped wheels of a compound bow make the weight increase rapidly, stay at peak weight for several inches, then drop into the valley.*

Stored Energy Comparison

When the force-draw curves of all three types of bows having the same peak weight are compared, then the stored energy relationship between them can be examined. Stored energy is determined by the square units of area between the force-draw curve and the horizontal draw weight axis of the graph. The most obvious feature of the comparison in Figure 7 is that the compound bow has a distinct advantage in storing energy. The recurve comes in second with a slight advantage over the longbow.

• *Fig. 7a. The stored energy of this longbow with peak weight of 50 pounds is 43 foot-pounds, which is represented by 516 square inches of shaded area under the force-draw curve.*

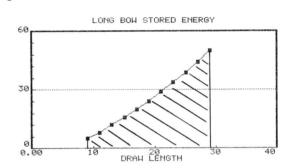

• *Fig. 7b. The stored energy of this recurve bow with peak weight of 50 pounds is 47 foot-pounds, represented by 564 square inches of shaded area under the force-draw curve.*

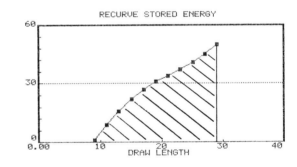

• *Fig. 7c. The stored energy of this compound with peak weight of 50 pounds is 52 foot-pounds, represented by 634 square inches of area under the force-draw curve.*

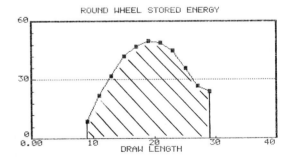

The compound bow gets this advantage in stored energy by using its short, stiff limb to reach peak weight soon after the draw cycle begins. The cam-shaped wheel on the compound bow does an even better job of storing energy since it gets to peak weight quicker and stays there longer than the round wheel (Fig. 8).

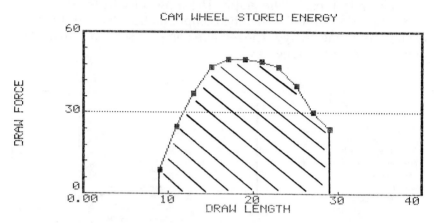

• *Fig. 8. This cam wheel compound bow with a peak weight of 50 pounds stores 56 foot-pounds of energy, represented by 672 square inches of shaded area under the force-draw curve.*

It would be easy to conclude, also, that the compound is faster than the other bows, but that may not be the case. Another facet of the bow as a machine — efficiency — comes into play and can minimize any effect extra stored energy may have. The dynamic efficiency of the bow may be so low that too much energy is needed to run all of the parts of the machine and little remains to be given to the arrow. This condition will greatly affect any conclusions that are to be made about which bow is the fastest and most effective.

Bow efficiency is the ratio of the energy the bow gives to the arrow compared to the energy stored in the bow. Most of the bows on the market today are between 50 percent and 85 percent efficient. This means that they give 50 percent to 85 percent of the stored energy in the limbs to the arrow as the arrow leaves the string.

The longbow and the recurve bow operate in the 60-85 percent efficiency range. Compounds operate in the 50-85 percent efficiency range. The best bows transfer about 80 percent of their stored energy to the arrow. Poorly designed compounds have been tested as giving only 50 percent of their energy to the arrow.

The measurement of a bow's efficiency begins with the making of the force-draw curve. Once the curve is made, the area under the

Force-Draw Curve

curve can be mathematically computed. To do this, the area under the curve can be divided into one-inch-wide rectangles as in Figure 9. The area of each rectangle is calculated and the sum of all the rectangular areas is found. In the given example, a compound bow with a peak weight of 50 pounds, round eccentric wheels, and a 29 inch draw length has a stored energy value of 57 foot-pounds.

The one-inch-wide rectangular areas are added and divided by 12 (inches in a foot) to yield foot-pounds of stored energy: (17 + 21 + 25 + 30 + 34 + 40 + 46 + 48 + 50 + 50 + 49 + 47 + 44 + 39 + 35 + 30 + 27 + 26 + 25) ÷ 12 = (683) ÷ 12 = 56.9 ft. lbs.

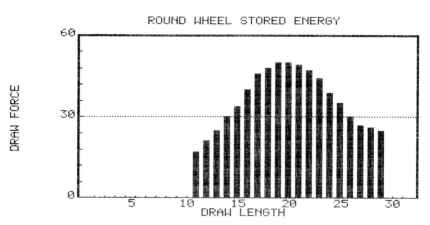

• *Fig. 9. This round wheel compound bow stores 57 foot-pounds of energy and gives a 500 grain arrow a velocity of 200 feet per second. The arrow has 44.42 foot-pounds of kinetic energy, which makes the bow 77.9 percent efficient.*

The next step in the efficiency measuring process is to shoot an arrow through a chronograph and record its velocity in feet per second. The velocity and weight of the arrow can then be used in the formula for kinetic energy:

$$K.E. = \frac{(W \text{ (grains)} \times V \times V)}{450,240}$$

Written out, this is Kinetic Energy equals the Weight of the arrow (in grains) times Velocity times Velocity, divided by 450,240.

This formula is not difficult to use. At least you now know how to calculate the energy of a moving arrow.

In the given example, the arrow weight is 500 grains and its velocity when the arrow leaves the bow is 200 feet per second. Applying the formula for kinetic energy, the arrow has 44.42 foot-pounds of energy.

The efficiency of this particular bow can now be determined by comparing the 44.42 foot-pounds of energy that the bow transferred to the arrow with the 57 foot-pounds of energy that was originally stored in the limbs of the bow. In other words, divide 44.42 by 57 to get the decimal value of .779 or 77.9 percent efficiency. This bow is a good example of what you will find with many of today's compound bows.

Some of the stored energy of the bow is used to run the machinery of the bow — any bow, every bow. In the given example, most of the 22.1 percent of the stored energy not given to the arrow was used to move the limbs, cables, string and wheel. A small percent of the energy not given to the arrow was lost in vibrations and friction.

A good recurve with the same efficiency — 77.9 percent —will usually shoot a slower arrow than a compound bow. A recurve with a peak weight of 50 pounds usually stores less than 50 foot pounds of energy. If 48 foot-pounds of stored energy are used and multiplied by the efficiency of .779 (77.9 percent), then the arrow would have only 37.4 foot-pounds of kinetic energy (Fig. 10). This means a significant difference in arrow velocity if the same arrow is being used. Also, since the recurve is slightly more efficient than the longbow, a longbow with the same peak weight will give a little less energy to the arrow, making it slightly slower.

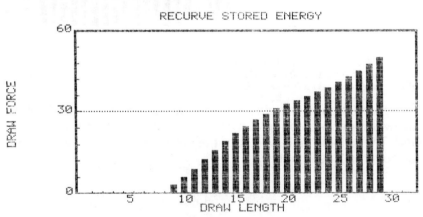

• Fig. 10. A recurve bow that is 77.9 percent efficient and stores 48 foot-pounds of energy will give the arrow 37.4 foot-pounds of kinetic energy.

Please remember that in these comparisons all bows have the same peak weight and draw length and the same arrow is being shot from each. If this were not the case, any comparison would be unfair.

One conclusion that **cannot** be made is that high efficiency automatically means high velocity. To get velocity, the bow must store a reasonable amount of energy. Then the bow must give most of that energy to the arrow. For instance, if a bow stores only 10 foot-pounds of energy and gives all of it to the arrow, the bow is 100 percent efficient but the arrow lands at your feet.

The Overdraw Arrow Rest and Arrow Velocity

Arrow velocity can be increased simply by decreasing the weight of the arrow. This can be done by shortening the arrow or by using a smaller diameter and thinner-walled arrow shaft, or a combination of these methods. Regardless of the method of making the arrow lighter in weight, the result usually is an increase in arrow speed because the stored energy of the bow has less arrow weight to move.

To accommodate the shorter arrow, you must relocate the arrow rest of the bow so it is closer to the bowstring. A bracket is mounted on the riser of the bow as shown in Figure 11. By mounting the arrow rest to this bracket and between the handle riser and the bowstring, you are able to use an arrow that is one to six inches shorter than the arrow normally used. The weight reduction factor for this shorter arrow is about 10 to 15 grains of weight per inch of arrow shaft removed. That's a decrease in weight of from 10 to 90 grains and an increase in arrow speed of as much as 20 feet per second.

• *Fig. 11. The overdraw arrow rest is mounted between the handle and string and allows the use of a shorter and lighter arrow. Never use an overdraw mount without a safety guard between the rest and your bow arm and hand.*

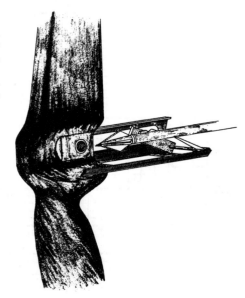

Because a shorter arrow is lighter in weight it tends to be stiffer. This fact may require you to increase draw weight or use an arrow that is smaller in diameter and/or has a thinner wall (compared to the usual matching rules) to achieve best arrow flight. The weaker spined and smaller sized arrow will give the greatest advantage in arrow speed and for that reason is the most chosen route to good arrow flight with the overdraw arrow rest.

By using a shorter, smaller diameter and thinner walled arrow shaft, you get the maximum that an overdraw rest has to offer. The weight reduction with the smaller and shorter arrow can be as much as 200 grains. Some archers are using arrows that weigh as little as 250 grains. Speeds for these arrows are in excess of 300 feet per second.

As is always the case in archery and bow tuning, a gain in one area means a sacrifice in another. The sacrifice with the overdraw is two-fold:

1) Shooting the light arrow causes the bow to shoot less efficiently;

2) Greater arrow rest movement due to torque in the grip area of the handle.

Both problems require attention so their side effects are minimized.

The large majority of bow reports found in publications show that

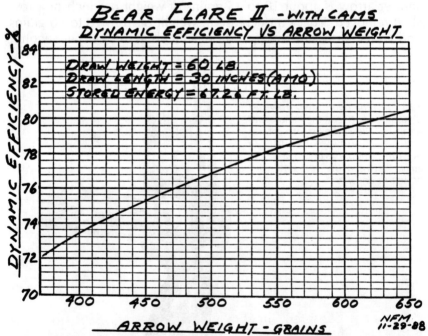

• Fig. 12. This bow dynamic efficiency chart by Norb Mullaney shows less bow efficiency when lighter arrows are shot and more bow efficiency for heavier arrows. This is the case with any bow.

a bow will transfer a greater percent of its stored energy to a heavy arrow than it will to a light arrow. That means that when a lighter arrow is shot from a bow, more of the stored energy is being lost to vibration and other parasitic effects. The lighter the arrow, the more energy is lost in the bow system, as shown in Figure 12. The limit of this reasoning would involve an arrow that has no weight and would cause all the stored energy of the bow to be lost. This is the case with a "dry fire". This condition, of course, can result in damage being done to the limbs, bowstring and cable system of the bow.

An arrow rest located at some point other than directly over the pressure point between the hand and handle riser will be greatly affected by any movement of the hand during the shot process. Figure 13 demonstrates the greater movement of the overdraw rest which may be three or four inches away from the grip or pressure point of the handle riser. This means that a slight upward, downward or sideways twisting of the hand on the grip will be exaggerated by the

• Fig. 13a. The top view of the overdraw rest shows the possible left/right rest movement caused by horizontal torque in the grip of the bow.

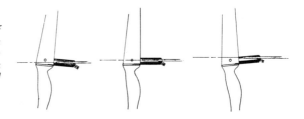

• Fig. 13b. A side view of the overdraw rest shows the possible up/down movement of the rest as vertical torque is applied to the grip of the handle.

length of the overdraw mounting bracket. The result is a greater divergence by the arrow from the intended path of flight.

Stable and consistent shooting form is a necessity if the overdraw is to be an advantage. To shoot the overdraw rest consistently, you must be willing to invest more time developing a stable bow arm and grip. Without that investment, you may experience less accuracy.

Remember, a fast miss is still a miss. The worst result is a non-vital hit on an animal.

Finally, the overdraw rest can shoot the lighter arrow at a faster speed, but the heavier arrow will have more kinetic energy, since the bow and arrow combination operates more efficiently. The faster arrow is a decided advantage when you are trying to estimate distance and hit the intended target. This applies well to long distance shooting at large animals and has been used successfully by many bowhunters. The lighter arrow, however, does not receive as much of the stored energy from a given bow as does a heavier arrow and does not have as much kinetic energy. Less kinetic energy usually means less penetration. The exception to this is the very small diameter carbon shafts. Because of the greatly reduced surface area and low drag effect of these shafts, the penetration they have can be greater than larger shafts with the same spine. Test the penetration of your overdraw arrangement at the distance you intend to use it. Be sure that you can make a vital hit. Take the time to do it right.

Chapter 3

Bow Fitting

Using The Bow At Its Designed Draw Length

The feel of the bow you intend to use is of the utmost importance
to tuning the bow. Without the proper feel in the bow, you cannot
reach your full potential nor can the bow give the best it has to offer.
Because the bow must feel good when you draw and shoot it, the
single most important concern in the tuning process is the draw length
of the bow and how it relates to your draw length.

Each style of bow has its own design characteristics as shown in
the force-draw curves presented in the preceding chapter. These draw
characteristics must be known if you intend to shoot the given bow
at its designed draw length. The recurve and longbows should be
ordered with the correct draw length, but in this case it is less critical
than for a compound bow. In the case of the compound bow, you
will set the draw length during the tuning process. Then and only
then can the bow be drawn and released from the proper position
and yield the best results.

For many longbows, particularly older ones, the force-draw curve
was very close to a straight line until the bow started to stack. Then

the force-draw curve curved upward at an increasing rate (Fig. 14). However, a well-designed longbow has a curve similar to that of a recurve bow, except that the rounded hump in the early stages of the draw is less pronounced. Stacking in a well designed longbow usually begins at a later stage in the draw than in a poorly designed longbow.

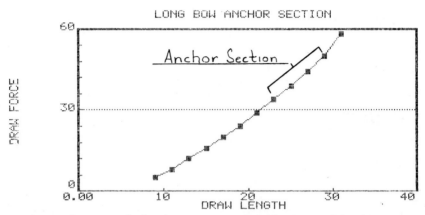

• Fig. 14. When using the longbow, you must be able to control the draw weight at your desired anchor point. The anchor should be at a position in the draw curve preceding any sharp increase or "stacking" of the draw weight.

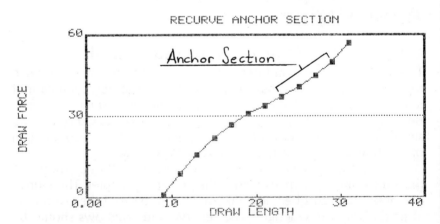

• Fig. 15. The recurve should be drawn to a point in the force-draw curve where the reflex limb tips have caused lesser increase in the rate of draw weight but before any stacking occurs.

Since the recurve bow has two phases to its draw cycle, you must understand both in order to get the most out of the bow. The first is the very fast increase in draw weight on the bowstring during the beginning of the draw cycle. The second occurs as the reflex limb tips begin to unbend. During this stage, as mentioned in the previous chapter, the increase in draw weight lessens and a softer feel on the bowstring results. It is in this softer region that you need to anchor and then release the bowstring (Fig. 15). If you anchor in front of this position, then you are not gaining full advantage of the reflex limbs, and if you anchor further back in the draw cycle you will experience a greater rate of increase in weight on the bowstring. In other words, if you do not anchor where the reflex is causing a lesser rate of increase in weight on the string, you might as well be shooting a longbow.

Longbows and recurves are not as critical with regard to matching the archer's draw length to the draw length of the bow as are compound bow types. The very nature of the force-draw characteristics of stick bows — the fact that there is no narrow and distinct "valley" in the force-draw curve permits wider latitude in the selection of draw length that is ideal for shooting a given bow.

All good recurves, and properly designed longbows, will have a "sweet spot" in the force-draw curve. In reality, this is more than a "spot" because it is usually several inches long. It is that portion of the force-draw curve that is essentially linear (straight line). That is, that range of draw length where the increase in draw weight is constant for a given increment of draw length.

For example, if the draw length is increased one inch, the draw weight will increase 2½ pounds — and this same 2½ pound increase will occur as the draw length is increased inch by inch. After that, the draw weight increase may move up to 3, 3½ or 4 pounds per inch of draw length as the bow begins to stack.

The ideal draw length for the bow is within this "sweet" area of the force-draw curve. Shooting from this range of draw length will offer the greatest consistency and the best "feel" to the bow.

The length and location of the "sweet spot" will be influenced by limb design, limb length, brace height, handle length, deflex or reflex and other factors. Overall length of the bow and the relationship of handle length to limb length have a decided influence on the location of the "sweet spot".

However, it is not as critical to shoot within the "sweet spot" of a stick bow as it is to stay in the valley of a compound bow.

The force-draw curve of the compound bow shows three phases in the draw cycle. First, the draw weight increases rapidly until it reaches peak weight. Next, the eccentric wheels cause a shift in weight from the bowstring to the power cables, and the weight on the bowstring decreases for some distance. This decrease does not continue forever. The size of the wheel or cam allows the weight to let off for a set distance. Beyond this distance, the force on the bowstring will begin to increase even more rapidly than in the beginning of the draw cycle. This third phase is called the wall, while the second phase is called the slope. The slope begins at peak weight and ends in the valley or point of lowest holding weight. It is in this valley that you need to anchor and release the compound bow (Fig. 16). The valley provides a region in the draw cycle where the force on the bowstring changes slowly and very little. If the bow is released when the force is in the valley, the arrow is given a smooth, accelerated start.

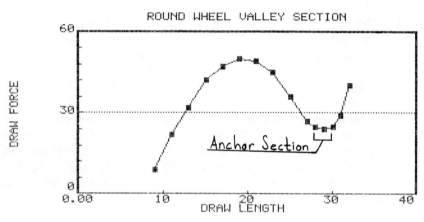

• *Fig. 16. The compound bow must be drawn to and released from the bottom of the "valley" of the force-draw curve. Releasing from any other position will result in less than optimum performance.*

Determining Your Draw Length

You must measure your true draw length so you can take better advantage of the bow you plan to use. The most accurate method of measuring your true draw length is to draw the bow of a friend who is about the same arm length as you. This must be done using the finger tab, glove or release aid you plan to use when you shoot.

After you have drawn the bow several times and feel somewhat comfortable, draw again with an arrow in the bow. When you reach the anchor point that seems best for you, have someone mark the arrow at the arrow rest mounting hole in the handle riser. This mark should be directly above the grip where your hand meets the deepest part of the handle (Fig. 17). The distance from this mark to the recess in the nock of the arrow is called the true draw length of the archer. It is a measure of your body size for the purpose of drawing a bow.

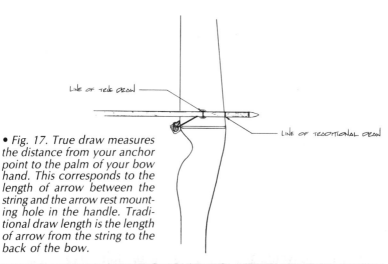

LINE OF TRUE DRAW

LINE OF TRADITIONAL DRAW

• *Fig. 17. True draw measures the distance from your anchor point to the palm of your bow hand. This corresponds to the length of arrow between the string and the arrow rest mounting hole in the handle. Traditional draw length is the length of arrow from the string to the back of the bow.*

• *Fig. 18. Measurement of the length of arrow between the string and the mark, corresponding to the rest mount hole in the handle, has been made.*

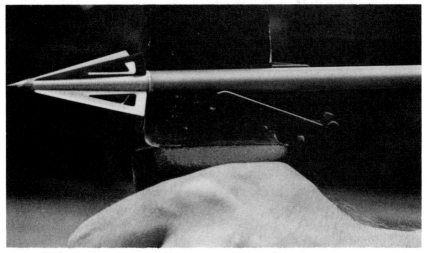

• *Fig. 19. The broadhead must not be drawn into the back of the bow. If it is, it may cause the arrow to fall off the rest, or the bottom blade may slice your top bow hand finger.*

Beware, most bow manufacturers do not advertise or take orders using true draw measurements. Instead, they use a traditional draw length which is slightly longer than true draw. The difference is the distance from the arrow rest mounting hole to the back (the side facing away from you) of the bow (Fig. 18). This adds, depending on the handle design, about 1-3/4 inches to the true draw measurement. The Archery Manufacturers Organization (AMO) has adopted the following standard:

Traditional Draw = True Draw + 1¾ Inches

If you are using the standard arrow rest mounting hole in the handle riser, then your arrow length must be at least as long as your traditional draw length. The purpose of this is to prevent the broadhead on your arrow from hitting the handle riser when you draw to full draw (Fig. 19). A shorter arrow may be used if the handle riser you are using has been designed with a cutout window around the arrow rest. This would allow space for the broadhead to be drawn beside the handle riser.

Throughout this process, remember that if you are using a release aid your true draw length is usually different from when you are using a finger tab or glove. This difference can be from a small fraction of an inch to as much as two inches, depending upon the release used and the anchor technique. The release acts as an extension of your fingers and will cause the string to be drawn less than when drawn without the release in hand. This also means that if you switch styles of shooting from release aid to fingers, you will have to make an adjustment to the draw length of a compound bow so you always will anchor in the middle of the valley.

Draw Length Adjustment Methods

As indicated in the previous section, the bow must have the same draw length as the person shooting it. This means that you must select the correct longbow or recurve bow to use. In the case of the compound bow, you must select the bow with the correct wheel size and also know how to adjust the draw length in small increments. The bow must fit the person using it so when that person is anchored at full draw, the bow is at the proper place in the draw cycle. If not, that person never will obtain the full potential from the bow or from himself.

In the case of the longbow and the recurve bow, draw length and the draw weight at that draw length are determined by the bowyer when the design of the bow is fixed. Limb thickness, limb width and limb length, among other factors, determine the draw weight needed to draw the bow to a given distance.

Here the term "tillering" can be used, since the limbs of the bows are shaved or filed so the desired bend, draw weight and shooting characteristics can be achieved. Upper and lower limbs may not be of identical thickness at each point of their length, because wood just doesn't grow to identical consistency throughout. Therefore, one of the limbs will need to be shaved or filed so it matches the other limb and they work smoothly together. The first way to determine that they are properly tillered is to measure the perpendicular distance from the bowstring to the bow handle at fade-out (bases of the upper and lower limbs).

With recurves, the tiller should be slightly more on the upper limb, which should be slightly weaker than the lower limb. This difference generally is somewhere around 1/8 inch. This is necessary because you are not holding the bow at its vertical center. You are holding the bow handle below center. The position of the grip and the position at which the arrow is placed require this difference in the limbs in order to have them act together dynamically.

You can adjust the draw length of a longbow or recurve in two ways — by replacing the present bowstring with a longer or shorter one or by twisting the bowstring now on the bow.

A shorter bowstring increases the brace height of the bow and increases the draw weight (from what it was at a given draw length). A longer string decreases the bow's brace height and decreases the draw weight (from what it was at a given draw length).

Too long a bowstring will cause the bow to become harsh and noisy. Too short a string will cause reduction in stored energy and therefore reduce arrow velocity.

Twisting the existing bowstring on the bow will change the draw length very little. Twisting a bowstring too many times puts too much stress on the strands and, in effect, weakens the bowstring. Conversely, untwisting the bowstring beyond the desired twist also weakens it, as well as lengthening it slightly.

The compound bow is a quite different machine. By changing wheel sizes, string lengths and cable lengths, the draw length and draw weight can be changed in large increments. This is why I can change one of my bows to fit my wife or my daughter. The phrase "one bow fits all" is more often true than not for the compound bow.

Since different wheel sizes can be used to change the draw length of the compound bow, most bow manufacturers make several sizes. These wheels have diameters in the range of 1½ inches to 3½ inches (Fig. 20). These sizes, coupled with bow axle to axle lengths of 44 inches to 50 inches, make draw lengths from 23 inches to 34 inches.

• *Fig. 20. Different wheel sizes from 1-1/2 to 2-1/2 inches allow bow manufacturers to build bows with draw lengths from 23 to 34 inches.*

The eccentric wheel system is the heart of the compound bow. It is the action of this wheel or cam which causes the three phases of the force-draw curve. Understanding the mechanics of the eccentric system will help explain why these three phases occur and ultimately how to adjust the draw length of the compound bow to fit you.

Because the axle of the eccentric is not in the center, the wheel or cam acts as a lever which has a changing leverage ratio. The point of maximum leverage is found by drawing a line from the axle hole of the wheel (Fig. 21), through the center of the wheel, to the opposite side of the wheel. This line locates that point on the edge of the wheel which is farthest from the axle hole. This point should be marked so its position can be noted during the three phases of the draw cycle.

• *Fig. 21. The line of maximum leverage for a round wheel extends from the axle hole through the center of the wheel and onto the far edge of the wheel.*

When the bow is at rest or in the braced position, the maximum leverage line is located near the limb. However, there is no significance in the location of the limb and its relationship to the line of leverage. As the bow is drawn toward peak weight, the maximum leverage line rotates toward the outside of the limb tips. As the bow reaches peak weight, the line will form a right angle with the limb tip. At this position, the leverage ratio between the string and the cables begins to place more load on the power cables.

The force on the bowstring decreases, but not forever. The diameter of the eccentric is limited in size and therefore will give let-off for only a limited length of the draw stroke. Larger wheels will give let-off over a greater length of draw than smaller wheels. Therefore, larger people need larger wheels so the "valley" or point of maximum let-off will occur when they are at full draw. Beyond this point in the draw cycle the string will again carry more and more of the force necessary to bend the limbs.

• *With a bow and arrow, the margin of error is small at the moment of truth. Well-set-up equipment helps reduce the odds.*

The next three illustrations make an important part of this book. Figure 22a shows the maximum leverage line just before reaching the valley. Figure 22b shows the maximum leverage line in the middle of the valley, and Figure 22c shows the line after the draw weight passes the valley. Should you continue drawing the bow beyond the middle of the valley, the draw weight will begin to increase sharply. This increase is so steep that some archers describe it as the "wall". Once the bow is drawn beyond the valley it begins working like a straight-limbed bow — the further you pull it, the greater the weight becomes.

• *Fig. 22a. Before reaching the valley, the end of the maximum leverage line has not yet reached the point where the string cable leaves the wheel.*

• *Fig. 22b. The middle of the valley occurs when the maximum leverage line reaches the point where the string cable leaves the wheel.*

• *Fig. 22c. After passing the middle of the valley, the maximum leverage line will be rolled past the point where the string cable leaves the wheel.*

Review Figure 22b. The leverage line through the wheel is ending at the point where the string cable is leaving the wheel. The wheel will not give you any mechanical advantage when drawn beyond this point. Therefore, the weight felt on the string has to increase rapidly.

For best performance, both wheels must be operating in synchronization. If one wheel is out of time with respect to the other, poor arrow flight and overall bad performance result. This condition is most often found in four-wheel compounds since the roll-over of each wheel can be independently adjusted. Two-wheel compounds are built with synchronized roll-over (Figs. 23a & 23b) which is retained as long as the cables do not slip in the eccentrics. Corrections for this condition are discussed in Chapter Four.

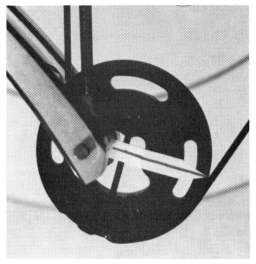

• *Fig. 23. Top and bottom wheels must roll the same amount at full draw. If they do not, maximum performance will not be attained. Wheel synchronization can be checked by examining both lines of maximum leverage.*

The cam wheel follows the same three basic stages as the round wheel. From the force-draw curve pictured (Fig. 24), you can see the upward slopes and the downward slope are much steeper, and the peak is wider. Although more energy is stored in the limbs by the cam, the valley is usually narrower.

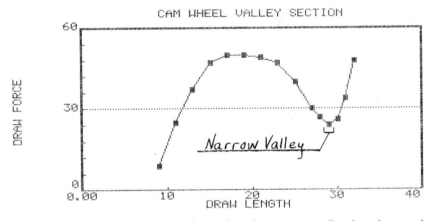

• Fig. 24. The cam wheel gives a wider peak and a narrower valley than the round wheel.

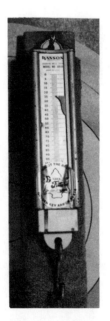

• Fig. 25. When the draw weight reaches a low point on the scale, the cam can be marked where the string cable leaves the cam.

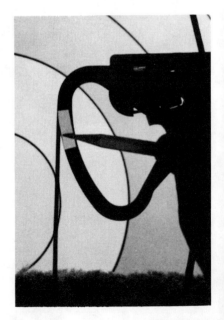

Bow Fitting

Drawing the line of maximum leverage through the cam is a bit more difficult than with the round wheel. We begin at the axle as before, but locating the center of the cam is the tricky part. Some cams have a mark or hole at the geometric center which will determine the line of maximum leverage. When no mark exists, you must rely on a scale to indicate when the weight reaches a low point in the middle of the valley (Fig. 25). Once you have found the middle of the valley, then you can draw the line of maximum leverage through the cam to the point on the cam where the string cable leaves the cam.

The pictures provided show the line of maximum leverage of three different cams (Figs. 26a, 26b, 26c) and a sequence of the line of maximum leverage before the cam reaches the valley (Fig. 27), in the valley (Fig. 28) and after the cam passes the valley (Fig. 29). These pictures show that the cam rotates through the same positions as the round wheel.

Most compound bow manufacturers make multiple-draw-length wheels. These wheels have two or three slots into which the cable can be placed in order to adjust draw length. The range of adjustment for these kinds of wheels is about three inches. This versatility means that you can better adjust the bow to fit your draw length, and the archery dealer needs to stock fewer bows to fit all of his customers.

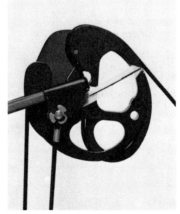

• Fig. 26. Here are three cams with markings for the line of maximum leverage. The top two are drawn to the middle of the valley, while the cam shown lower left is in the brace position.

• Fig. 27. This is the maximum leverage line before reaching the valley.

• Fig. 28. When the bow is drawn to the middle of the valley, the maximum leverage line points to the string cable leaving the edge of the wheel.

• Fig. 29. Beyond the middle of the valley, the maximum leverage line rolls past the point where the string cable leaves the wheel.

The multiple draw length slots in an eccentric wheel allow one wheel to provide the force-draw curves of several different sizes of wheels (Fig. 30). Each slot usually provides a change of about one inch in draw length. A given tri-draw wheel, for example, could provide the shooter with a valley at 29 inches or 30 inches or 31 inches, depending upon the slot used. The shortest draw length on these wheels is obtained by placing the cables in the slots toward the outside of the bow as shown in Figure 31. The longest draw length is obtained by placing the cables in the slots toward the inside of the bow (Fig. 32). The same bow will give the three force-draw curves in the diagram.

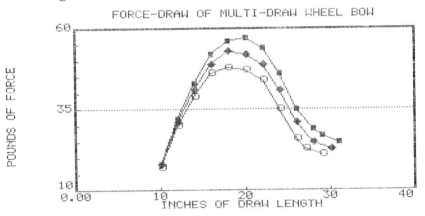

• Fig. 30. The multiple-draw wheel can be adjusted to give three or more different force-draw curves.

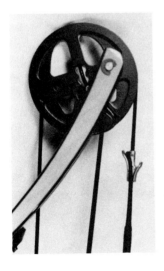
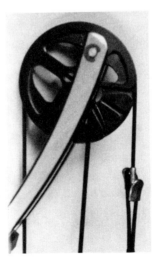

• Fig. 31. The short draw position is obtained by placing the cables in the slots farthest from the middle of the bow, shown far left.

• Fig. 32. The long draw position is obtained by placing the cables in the inner slots, shown in the photo to immediate left.

As the draw length is increased, several characteristics of the bow system change. When the cables are moved to a slot for longer draw length, the limb bend at full draw is increased. This translates into about five pounds more added peak weight for each inch of draw length added. The amount of let-off will also increase. The long draw length position of the multiple draw wheel will have about 10 percent more let-off than the short draw length.

Many of the bows with multiple-draw-length wheels will show their best performance when set in the short or medium draw lengths. The reasons for this are increased pre-bend in the limbs in the shorter draw lengths and the lower let-off. Both of these characteristics make the cable system tighter and more consistent.

Wheel Modules For Draw Length Adjustment

Another effective way to adjust draw length is to employ a removable module on the eccentric. This is most often done with cam wheels. The module is made in several different sizes and designed so it can be removed from the cam and replaced with a module of a different size (Fig. 33). The module is located on the smaller side, or power side, of the cam. Since the cable system is not in contact with the module when the bow is in the brace position, the module easily can be removed by loosening one or two screws. The module controls the way the power cable wraps around the cam, therefore it controls the shape of the force-draw curve. The module can be used to give the cam the force-draw curve of a round wheel as well as to lengthen or shorten the draw length.

• *Fig. 33. Modules for three draw lengths accompany this cam. Two different styles of modules give the wheel a true cam force-draw curve or a round wheel force-draw curve.*

• *Fig. 34. The yoke button in the cable system can be used to make minor adjustments to draw length as well as to modify wheel synchronization.*

Another method of adjusting the draw length of the compound is to utilize a small slotted wheel or yoke button, located in the cable system (Fig. 34). This button controls the length of the return or power cable. By making the cable ¹⁄₁₆ or ⅛ inch shorter, the draw length is increased by about ⅛ to ¼ inch. When the cable is made longer using the button adjustments, the draw length is going to be shorter. These adjustments are small and are used to fine tune the bow's draw length to match yours.

Yoke buttons also can be used to adjust the timing of the roll-over of the eccentric wheels. This can be done by changing only one of the yoke buttons. In other words, change one power (inner) cable only. Please remember that the compound works best if both wheels are rolling over in synchronization. When they don't, erratic arrow flight results.

Changing string length of the compound bow is another method used to alter draw length. By placing a shorter string on a compound, the draw length can be decreased. Under this condition the wheels are advanced into the draw cycle. Therefore, you do not have to draw the string as far to get to the middle of the valley. A side effect of this draw length shortening is the loss of some peak weight.

Here's a rule of thumb to follow: For each inch of decrease in draw length, the peak weight will drop about four or five pounds. The reverse is true if the draw length is increased by using a longer string: One inch longer draw length obtained by using a longer string gives a draw weight increase of four to five pounds. These numbers, of course, vary with different size wheels and different size limbs but will be in the ball park for all bows.

When a shorter string is put on a compound bow, the pre-bend of the limbs is increased. For that reason you must be careful not to exceed the manufacturer's standards for the amount of total bend to be given the limbs. When a longer string is installed on the compound, the reverse happens and pre-bend is decreased and another condition must be guarded against. That is the possible overlap of cable on the eccentric wheel or cam (Fig. 35). This overlap occurs when the cable is too long. The side effects of the overlap are increased cable wear at the point of overlap, porpoising arrow flight as the cable overlaps itself on the wheel at the end of each shot, and increased noise from cable slap.

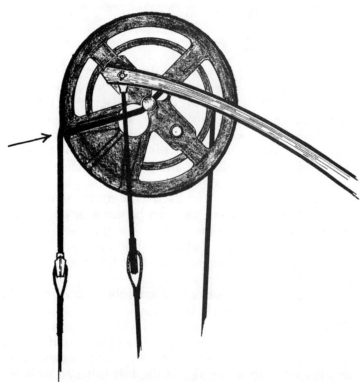

• Fig. 35. When cable lengths are altered or a longer bowstring is used, the cables must be checked to be sure they do not overlap as shown in this sketch.

Chapter 4

The Broadhead And
Its Effects On Arrow Flight

Most of the shooting we do as bowhunters is done with field points. The practice in the back yard, the animal target rounds and 3-D animal rounds at the local club are all shot with field points. Many bowhunters are involved in indoor leagues during the winter months and hone their shooting skills using field or target points. Some bowhunters participate in outdoor competitive rounds sanctioned by national or state archery associations. These rounds can be shot with field points, hunting weight arrows, and five fixed pins on your sight or no sight at all, if you are so inclined.

The more practice and competitive experience you can get, the better shooter you should be, all other things being equal. Obviously, everyone has his or her upper limit of shooting ability, and successful shooting is a combination of mental control, ability, and properly set up and tuned equipment. Some people say good shooting, of any kind, is 95 percent mental. That's a good thing to keep in mind, no pun intended. Mental control and positive thinking work wonders.

You still must have your equipment set up and tuned right, but you cannot be quick to blame the equipment every time a glitch develops. If you don't have confidence in your equipment setup and tuning skills, you really don't have confidence in yourself regarding your archery equipment, its performance and your archery abilities.

Competitive shooting places you under moments of stress, high stress. Competitive shooting tests your shooting form, your mental outlook and control, your archery equipment and your tuning skills.

Bowhunting obviously has its moments of stress, too. Most likely, the larger the trophy animal standing within shooting range, the more stress you will place yourself under.

During stress, we all either blow our cool or respond by doing what we have practiced the most and trained our subconscious and our muscles to do. With plenty of shooting practice — of the right kinds of practice for all bowhunting shot situations and conditions — you will have confidence in your equipment, your setup, your tuning and your ability to make it function properly at all times. If you haven't practiced enough and haven't practiced the right shots, then anything can happen. When the worst thing can happen, it usually does.

Before speaking of the right kinds of bowhunting shooting practice, which will be covered in a later chapter, we need to look at one other vitally important aspect of shooting practice. Not the shooting itself on a shot by shot basis, but the fact that there's a lot more to being a good bowhunter than being a good shot. In fact, **never place yourself in the position of using shooting skills as a crutch to cover up for lack of scouting or inability to put yourself in a high-percentage shot situation.** Just because you're deadly to 70 yards, for instance, on the target range, doesn't mean that you should shoot at any and all game seen within 70 yards. Some animals can smell you, unseen twigs can bump your arrow astray, your yardage estimate can be wrong, the animal may decide to move just as you release, unseen obstructions may be lurking in the arrow's trajectory, etc.

You're bowHUNTING, and your goal is to place yourself in a high-percentage shot situation at an unalarmed game animal. That is a situation with minimal stress, or as minimal as stress is going to be when a bowhunter and a game animal are involved. If you're not able to do that, you'll always be in a stressed situation — the animal won't be as close as it could be because you're out of position, the animal may have had a whiff of your scent, you may get a glimpse only of part of the animal, the animal may be moving instead of standing or walking, etc.

A good hunter who also is an excellent shot is an effective bowhunter. A good shot who is a poor hunter is going to shoot at

• *Set up for high-percentage shots. Don't try to let good shooting skills become a crutch for under-developed hunting skills, because they cannot.*

animals he or she should not shoot at and will hit, quite possibly poorly, some of those animals which should not even have been shot at.

(Editor's Note: From our experience, good archery shots wound —either superficially or fatally — more game than poor shots. Bowhunters who are poor shots either don't shoot or miss the shot. Bowhunters who are good shots, especially if they haven't developed their hunting skills enough, have understandable confidence in their shooting skills and may not be as aware as they should be of what are and are not high-percentage shots, or can't get themselves into the best position for a high-percentage shot. These conditions can lead to low-percentage shots being taken. This leads to some kills but a lot more unnecessarily wounded animals. That is the crutch of highly developed shooting skills. This situation shouldn't happen, but it does. We all can, however, do everything possible to prevent such situations from arising. We hope this commentary here and this book itself will help in reaching that goal.)

Now that I have you pumped up to practice a lot and do the necessary things to make yourself a good bowHUNTER, I must tell you that you have one more obstacle to deal with — the broadhead — before you are ready to complete any hunting shot. We do so much shooting during the year with field points, and just when we seem to have everything figured out we have to put all those broadhead blades on the front of our arrows. That's what this book is all about.

What's different about the arrow when the broadhead is installed? Should it hit the same place as field points? Should you really shoot broadheads in June or wait until the week before season?

This chapter deals with the physical properties of broadheads and how they must be handled so you can hit what you aim at when it really counts.

• Hitting what you aim at when it really counts results in smiles, meat for the table and great memories.

Broadhead Effects on Arrow Flight

The Field Point And Its Effects On The Arrow

Although the field point has no blades to steer the arrow, it still has an effect on the way the arrow flies. If you don't believe that, remove one and shoot the arrow. The result won't be pretty. The field point, because of its weight, changes the spine or bending characteristics of the arrow. Different weight points (Fig. 36) will change the trajectory of the arrow, cause the arrow to bend differently as it is shot and hit the target at a different location.

• *Fig. 36. Arrow points come in several weights, shapes and styles, and each affects the action of the arrow differently as it is shot.*

Since every arrow bends as it is being propelled by the string, understanding and controlling the bend is important. A brief description of what happens to an arrow as it is pushed by the string and, ultimately, releases from the string is necessary at this point.

The "Archer's Paradox" or puzzle for the longbow is described by Paul E. Klopsteg in "Archery: The Technical Side", 1947. If a bow is drawn, the nocked arrow aimed, and then the bow let back down to brace height without moving the handle, Klopsteg notes that "The axis of the arrow therefore points very appreciably —perhaps five degrees to seven degrees — to the left of where it is aimed. (Editor's Note: For a right-hand shooter) Now, if all conditions are kept as they were except that the arrow is fully drawn and loosed in the regular manner, it will fly accurately to its mark."

The paradox or puzzle lies in the fact that the arrow does not fly to the left as it was pointed before being drawn, but instead goes where it is aimed at full draw. Figures 37 and 38 show the paradox situation.

The only answer to this puzzle is the fact that the arrow bends as the force of the bowstring is applied to it. This force on the end of the slender column of the arrow, combined with the transverse forces (sideways, and up and down) which are input from the bowstring, pressure point and arrow rest, cause the arrow shaft to bend. Once the arrow is bent, being elastic it immediately starts to recover and

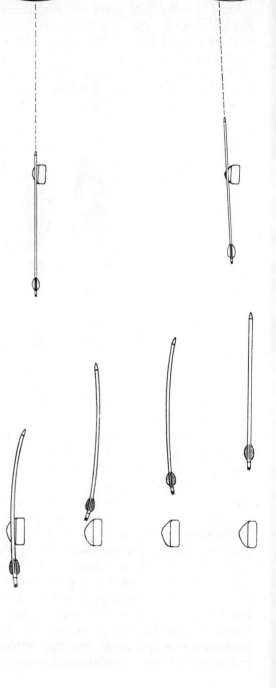

• Fig. 37. Near right illustration. Longbow at full draw. At full draw the arrow is aimed at the target and will hit the target when shot.

• Fig. 38. Far right illustration. Longbow at brace. When the arrow is let down, but the handle not moved, the arrow will point to the left of the target.

• Fig. 39. Below, this is the probable sequence of bending that an arrow experiences as it is shot around the handle of a wood-handle recurve bow and tries to stabilize in flight.

doesn't stop bending when it comes back to a straight position. Inertia causes it to bend in the opposite direction. These bending cycles are termed the "archer's paradox" and are necessary for the arrow to clear the handle and the arrow rest.

These bending cycles dampen quickly, but the length of time they persist depends on the stiffness of the arrow, its weight and the distribution of that weight. Figure 39 shows the top view of a typical sequence of events as the arrow is released.

The bending of the arrow must be timed correctly so it does not strike the handle of the bow as it passes. This is where point weight, arrow material, arrow length, arrow diameter and wall thickness become crucial. Heavier points and/or heavier fletches cause a shaft to be more flexible. Larger diameter and thicker walled shafts bend less because they are stiffer. **The right combination is a must for good arrow flight and good groups.**

Metal handles on bows, because of their greater strength, permit the bow to be cut more centershot than is the case with wood or other types of handles. When the arrow is nocked on a centershot bow, it can be pointed directly at the target when the bow is at brace height as well as when it is at full draw. It is easy to understand why this arrow will fly directly to the intended target.

It is considerably easier to select an arrow of proper spine for a centershot bow than for a bow that is not centershot. Centershot bows have a much greater tolerance for arrow spine than do non-centershot bows because the requirement for perfectly matched spine is not as great.

The bottom line here is that the spine of the arrow must always be matched to the bow system regardless of the type of system. How to do this is not dealt with in this chapter but is explained in the next chapter on actual tuning procedures. For now, it is sufficient to know that bending occurs and is affected by the point weight, shaft size and shaft length.

Broadhead Effects On Arrow Flight

Like the field point weight, the broadhead weight will change the spine of the arrow. The heavier the point, the weaker the effective spine of the arrow will be. The lighter the point, the stiffer the arrow shaft will act. So, as far as the weight is concerned, both field points and broadheads have the same effect on the arrow shaft, except for the location of the center of gravity of the point. On a broadhead, the center of gravity generally is further forward than on a field point. This affects the dynamic spine of the arrow, making it act less stiff.

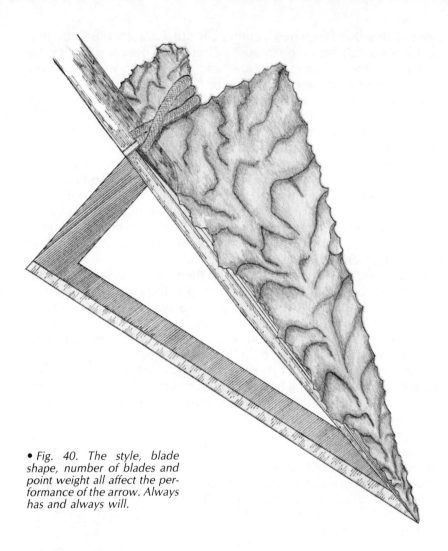

• Fig. 40. The style, blade shape, number of blades and point weight all affect the performance of the arrow. Always has and always will.

Point weight is where the similarity ends. The broadhead with its blades acting like forward rudders has an entirely different effect in the realm of aerodynamics. This effect can be likened to that of a racing boat which has been well tuned to slip through the water. The rudder is in the rear of the boat and makes the boat easy to control. Then another rudder is added to the front of the boat and, suddenly, the pilot must undertake a whole new set of steering actions to guide the boat. The same is true of the bowhunter trying to tune the arrow with a broadhead on the front end.

The boat with two rudders and the arrow with a broadhead experience a front versus rear steering problem. The end that wins this battle determines the direction the arrow flies. The following sections describe the causes of this steering problem for broadheads and how they can either be avoided or dealt with.

A) BLADE SURFACE

Simple logic dictates that the larger the blades on the broadhead the more that broadhead will try to steer the arrow. The same is true when more blades are added to the broadhead (Fig. 41). The cause of the problem is the transverse air pressure created on the surface area of the blades of the broadhead. The more square inches of area on the blades, the more transverse air pressure they will have and the more likely the blades are going to steer the arrow.

• Fig. 41. The total area of the three blades on this broadhead is 3 x (1/2 x 1.6 x 0.41) = 0.984 square inches.

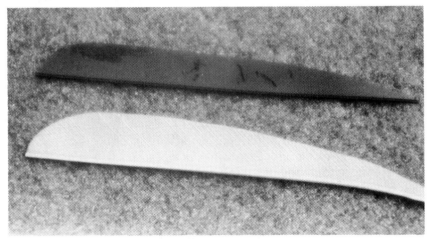

• Fig. 42. The surface area of a typical 4-1/2-inch fletch is 1.56 square inches. Three fletches on a shaft would give a total of 4.68 square inches of surface area.

To overcome the steering effect of the blades, fletching is added to the back end of the arrow shaft. The more and larger the fletching, the more likely the back will steer the arrow. The battle for control of the arrow is won, in part, by the end with the most square inches of surface area (Fig. 42). Surface area alone is not the total answer to control. The distance of the center of pressure of that area from the center of gravity of the entire arrow also is an important factor. The greater the distance from the center of gravity, the more effective is the control provided by the surface area.

One side effect that must be kept in mind is that the more surface area on the fletching and on the blades of the broadhead, the quicker the arrow will slow down. So, the arrow builder and bow tuner must make some trade-offs to obtain the best of both worlds. The primary concern must be the quality of arrow flight. The broadhead must be flying straight when it meets the target so maximum penetration will result. A super-fast broadhead that hits on its side will do two things — enrage you and startle the animal it was shot at. It sure won't penetrate.

B) NUMBER OF BLADES AND FLETCHES

The number of blades on the broadhead does not have to equal the number of fletches on the back of the arrow. Remember, it is the square inches of surface area which count. That means that four, five or even six blades can be used on the broadhead if enough surface area is on the fletching on the back end of the shaft. The number of fletches often exceeds the number of blades so the shooter can be certain the arrow will hit where it is aimed.

C) TYPE OF FLETCHING

The type of fletching you choose — feathers or plastic vanes — is a personal decision.

Feathers have more surface drag than do vanes of equal size. This is due to the ridges on the surface of the feather causing air turbulence as the feather moves through the air. This characteristic of feather fletching is why many broadhead flight problems can be overcome by using feathers. The additional surface drag of the feathers will stabilize the arrow sooner than vanes of equal size (Fig. 43). Feathers also are more forgiving of tuning or shooting form errors. A feather fletch will flatten when it hits an arrow rest or sight window, causing little or no bump to the arrow and thus being less likely to nudge the arrow out of good or acceptable launch and subsequent flight. For these two reasons, feathers may be the preferred choice if you are a bit uncertain of your fine tuning efforts and shooting form, or even if you are certain of them.

On the other hand, a quiverful of feather fletched arrows can be

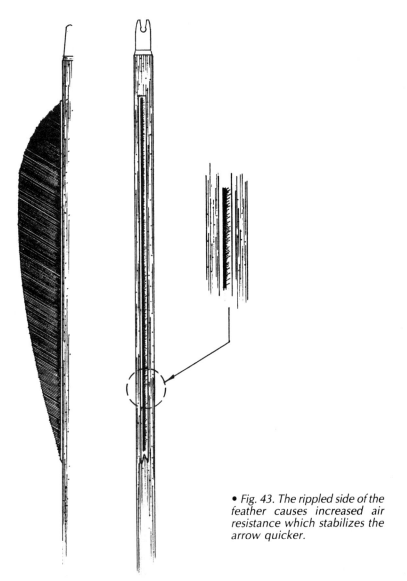

• Fig. 43. The rippled side of the feather causes increased air resistance which stabilizes the arrow quicker.

noisy when bumped; feathers are more expensive than vanes, and they tend to collapse when wet, which reduces the rudder effect. (But they can be treated with fly dope to make them water resistant.)

Vanes have about the same surface drag wet or dry; they are quiet in the quiver; they are less expensive, and they don't absorb water. They will do the job of stabilizing an arrow even with large broadheads.

Feathers can sustain more damage than vanes and still be effective.

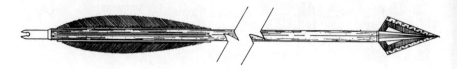

• Fig. 44. The blades of the broadhead do not have to be aligned with the fletching as shown in this drawing, but it sure doesn't hurt, either.

D) BLADE POSITION ON THE SHAFT

An old hunter's tale has always dictated that the blades of a broadhead must be aligned with the fletching. In other words, the three blades of a three-blade broadhead should be rotated on the shaft so they match the three fletches on the rear of the shaft (Fig. 44).

A theoretical aerodynamic study by Larry Luterman shows that there is some truth to this and that there is one or more best positions for alignment of broadhead blades and fletching. In fact, the difference between the best alignment and the poorest alignment, relative to total control of the arrow in the full 360 degrees around its axis, can be as much as 39 percent.

However, this factor is far less significant when the fletching provides good, positive control as it is supposed to do.

If, after progressing through the tuning process, you are still experiencing poor flight, it is likely that the problem is one or more of the following:

- Too weak or too stiff arrow spine;
- Too little surface area on the fletches;
- Contact between the fletching and the arrow rest;
- Improper roll-over of the eccentrics;
- Broadheads which are not mounted straight with the shaft.

The last of these problems can be dealt with in this section, while the others will be discussed in later chapters. Illustration 45 shows a broadhead ferrule or point that is not mounted straight with the shaft. If the point is not mounted properly on the shaft, then the blades will have one side pushing against the air instead of the leading edge cutting through it. The result is a broadhead that planes in one direction. If each of your arrows has its point bent in a different direction, then each arrow will plane differently. Groups are almost impossible under these conditions.

The cause of this problem is not necessarily the fault of the manufacturer. Several variables enter the situation when you are installing a broadhead.

1) The arrow first must be cut off perpendicular to the length of the shaft.

2) Next, the insert must fit properly and also have its end perpendicular to the length of the shaft.

3) Third, the ferrule must join correctly with the insert. If any one of these conditions is not met, then broadheads may fly in a direction other than the one in which they are aimed.

Rubber "O" rings are available through many manufacturers to help create a more precise fit between the insert and the ferrule. If that doesn't help, then you must physically straighten the point on the shaft. The straightness of the point can be checked by rolling the arrow on a short piece of two-inch by four-inch board. If the point is not straight with the shaft, it will appear to wobble as the arrow is rolled.

• Fig. 45. The point or ferrule must be mounted so it is in line with the arrow shaft. If it isn't, as illustrated here, then the arrow will plane to one side.

• Fig. 46. Rolling an arrow in an arrow straightener is a good method for locating ferrule points that are not in line with the arrow shaft. The tip will appear to wobble.

Rolling an arrow in an arrow straightener works better than using a board for this small job (Fig. 46). If the point doesn't wobble, you can assume it is straight with the shaft.

Because you have made certain all your arrows are straight and all the points are straight on the shafts, you can begin shooting them. Rotating the blades to match the fletching is less important since the square inches of surface area on the fletching can now work properly to stabilize the arrow and broadhead. I can't stress enough how important and how overlooked this step is in broadhead preparation. **Other than adjusting the draw length of the bow correctly to fit the archer, point straightening may be the most important activity in tuning broadheads.**

E) BLADE SHAPE

The actual shape of the blades on the broadhead has some bearing on the flight characteristics. Since the square inches of surface area is the determining factor in how much the broadhead will plane away from its intended direction, reducing the area by cutting vents in the blades will help reduce the planing. Some broadhead models accomplish this by making the broadhead very short with steeply angled blades (Fig. 47). This gives the same width cut of longer models but with less surface area. Whenever the surface area is reduced, then the broadhead generally is easier to tune.

• *Fig. 47. A short blade with a steeply angled cutting edge can reduce the surface area but not the width of cut. Vented blades can also reduce the surface area exposed to the air.*

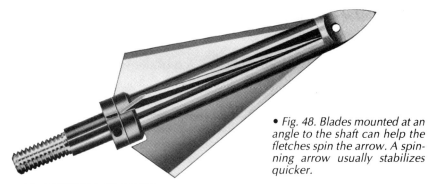

• *Fig. 48. Blades mounted at an angle to the shaft can help the fletches spin the arrow. A spinning arrow usually stabilizes quicker.*

F) ANGLED BLADES

Several manufacturers are making blades that are installed at an angle to the shaft (Fig. 48). This angle matches the angle of the fletching. The objective is to utilize the planing effects of the blades to help spin and stabilize the arrow. That means that if the fletching is left helical or straight with a slight angle to the left, then the blades of the broadhead must be angled to the left. Under this condition, the blades will help rotate the arrow on its axis in the same direction as the fletching. As long as the point is installed straight on the shaft, the angled blades will help stabilize the arrow.

G) NOCK FIT

The tightness with which the nock fits on the string is of great importance. If the nock fits too tightly, then the arrow may have a tendency to act stiffer than it should (Fig. 49). The nock end of the arrow may tend to stay too close to the handle riser of the bow and strike the side of the sight window as it passes by the arrow rest.

When the nock fits too loosely, the arrow may fly inconsistently. The string will not react the same on each shot if the fit is loose. When the arrow falls off the string, occasionally the nocks are not tight enough on the string.

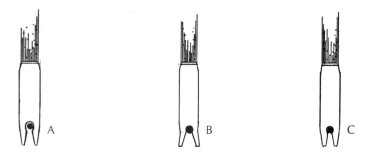

• *Fig. 49. Nock fit must not be too loose as in A or too tight as in B.*

A simple method of testing the fit is to hold the bow pointed downward. Snap the nock of the arrow on the string and let the arrow hang pointed downward. A tap on the string with the fingers should be enough to make the nock come loose. You should also be able to slide the nock up and down the string after it has been snapped onto the string.

If the arrow won't stay on the bowstring or it won't come off when the string is tapped with your fingers, select another nock size.

A bowstring with a different number of strands than the bowstring you are now using will also alter nock fit. For instance, if you have been shooting a 16-strand string and change to a 14-strand or 18-strand string, the nock fit may be improper.

H) CONCLUSION

The broadhead-equipped arrow is not a simple projectile. It requires knowledge and time to make it reach its intended target. With the aforementioned tuning tips, the results you get from shooting broadheads should improve. The only ingredient missing now is the time needed to make it happen.

Chapter 5

Arrow Rest Selection

The selection of an arrow rest for many early bows was easy. You were born with it. The arrow rest was the knuckle of your index finger on your bow hand. The arrow rested against the bow handle and on the knuckle. (An old friend, the late Fred Bear, shot his longbows and, later, recurve bows this way.) From this position, the bow was drawn and the arrow released with great accuracy and some pain. Turkish archers used a device called a siper which strapped to their bow hand and protected them from the arrow — the fletching, actually — as well as giving solid support to the arrow. Eventually, the longbow and then the recurve were constructed so they had a small shelf on which the arrow was rested. It worked, and the selection of a properly spined arrow was the major tuning technique used. There wasn't much else to do because little else was needed, other than being sure the nocks were aligned on the wooden shafts to match the wood grain so the shafts would bend properly when shot, and being sure the broadheads were aligned straight with the shaft. The arrow had to bend the correct amount so it would pass around the handle without hitting the handle or the shelf.

When I started shooting in the late 1950s, arrow rests consisted of small brushes or tightly grouped feathers for the under support of the arrow. The side support was usually several layers of leather build out from the bow handle so the arrow would pass by the handle cleanly.

The wood handle riser on most recurves and some compounds does not lend itself to a great amount of centershot adjustment. To maintain the strength of the handle, the center line of the handle must not be cut away. Such a cut would lead to handle failure. Therefore, there was no need for many of the rests on the market today. Instead, the size of arrow used was the main ingredient in the tuning process.

As handle materials became stronger and sight windows could be cut deeper, the arrow could be placed much closer to or directly over the center line of the grip (Fig. 50). Under this condition, greater accuracy was achievable with rests that would give way to the arrow. Plastic rests with support arms that moved laterally and vertically became popular, and soon after that came the cushion plunger.

• *Fig. 50. The latest handle designs allow the arrow to be placed directly over the center of the grip. They (the designs) also allow enough space for a broadhead to be drawn through the handle on an overdraw rest.*

The advent of the metal handle and the compound bow have led to the invention of arrow rests that take advantage of the complete centershot alignment of the arrow. The compound bow, I believe, causes a different kind of reaction in the arrow when the bowstring is released, and this reaction has need of a different kind of support from the arrow rest. This support must be yielding as much vertically as horizontally. The amount of bend tension in both directions is critical to achieving good arrow flight for arrows equipped with broadheads.

Centershot Alignment Of The Arrow

The center of pressure between your hand and the bow handle determines the center line of the bow system. The arrow will try to shoot through this center line of pressure, and the arrow rest must be aligned accordingly. When the arrow is not in this center line, the arrow and rest combination will not react to one another as well as they should. Arrow flight problems may result. Groups will not be as tight as they would be with better alignment.

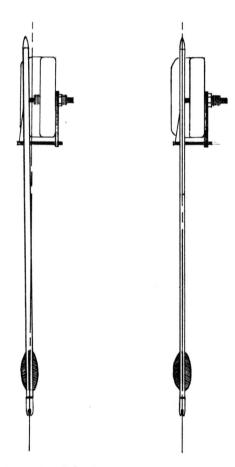

• Fig. 51. This drawing, far left, shows an arrow resting just to the left or outside of the center line of the grip.

• Fig. 52. Most release shooters adjust their arrow rests so the arrow is in the center line of the grip, as shown in illustration to the immediate left.

Many finger shooters will adjust their arrow rest to the left or right so the center of the arrow rests slightly to the outside of the center of pressure (Fig. 51). This means that right-handed shooters will have an arrow resting to the left of the center line of pressure while left-handed shooters will adjust until the center of their arrow rests slightly to the right of center. Two-time Olympic Gold Medalist Darrell Pace uses this centershot alignment for his recurve bows. He recommends this position as the starting location of the arrow rest for bow tuning. This is not a "set in cement" rule, and you may want to adjust your arrow so it rests on the center line of pressure at the start of the tuning process and change it while tuning.

The majority of release shooters move their arrow rests left or right until the arrow is resting in the center line of pressure (Fig. 52). The arrow tends to leave the compound with very little bending when shot with a release aid and almost always flies best when shot through the center of pressure. From this location, I seldom move the center-shot adjustment.

Some pros, however, do make centershot adjustments with their coiled-spring-type rests or V'eed launcher-type rests. Small left/right adjustments in the position of the arrow rest can sometimes affect the groups. Even small forward/rearward adjustments in the rest location can sometimes change the grouping ability of the bow. This should be tested at long range to better see the results. This is why some overdraws work well and some don't; by moving your arrow rest back an inch or so, sometimes the arrows — without cutting them shorter — will group better.

Rest Types

There are two major types of arrow rests. For want of better names, they can be called "shoot around" arrow rests and "shoot through" arrow rests. The shoot-around rest (Fig. 53) requires that the arrow bend around or move to the left side (for right-handed shooters) of the rest as it passes the handle riser. This is an acceptable procedure since most arrows do some kind of bending or vibrating as they pass by the arrow rest. The shoot-through rest (Fig. 54) provides support on the side of the arrow and also on the bottom of the arrow. This allows the bottom hen fletch of the arrow to pass between the two supports of the rest.

Both arrow rest types have their advantages and disadvantages. The shoot-through offers the capability of independent tension or pressure adjustment but does allow the arrow to fall between the two supports of the rest if the rest is not set up properly. The shoot-around

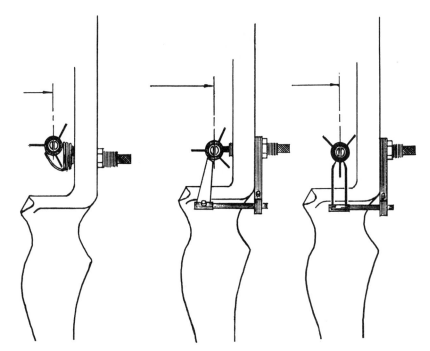

• Fig. 53. The shoot-around arrow rest requires the bottom hen fletch to pass around the bottom support arm of the rest.

• Fig. 54. The shoot-through arrow rest requires the bottom hen fletch to pass through the space between the side support and the bottom support launcher.

rest offers simplicity and durability but does not give much tension adjustment capability. You try different arrow rests until you find the combination that works best with your arrows and bow system.

Arrow rest selection is an ongoing process. Each bow you use may shoot better with a different rest than another bow you have owned. You and your shooting form may change during the weeks you spend practicing. In this case, an arrow rest change may be necessary to improve the grouping from your bow. A change in arrow sizes may also require a change in arrow rests. Don't change arrow rests every time a problem arises, but do be aware that a change in rests can bring about better groups if the conditions are right.

The Overdraw Arrow Rest

The overdraw arrow rest's (Fig. 55) sole purpose is to allow the shooting of shorter and lighter arrows in an effort to increase arrow velocity.

• Fig. 55. Most overdraw mounts will accept any of the arrow rests on the market. If you use an overdraw, be sure to install a guard between the mount bracket and your hand.

Most of the arrow rests on the market today can be placed on an overdraw mounting bracket. Some modification may be necessary to get your favorite rest on a safe overdraw mount, but generally it can be done. Because the overdraw mount allows the broadhead to be drawn over and behind the bow hand, safety is a big concern. A guard should be part of the mounting bracket. This guard should be attached so it is between the arrow point and your bow arm and hand. If the arrow comes off the arrow rest, then the guard will be there to prevent the arrow point from hitting arm or hand.

Don't use the overdraw rest without the guard installed. Don't spend part of the hunting season having a broadhead removed from your forearm, or various parts of your forearm being reattached to each other.

Chapter 6

Tuning With Field Points

Fine tuning a hunting bow begins with three phases of field point shooting. The first phase uses the powder test to check and correct fletch contact with the arrow rest. The second phase establishes good short range arrow flight by utilizing the paper test. Last, shoot-testing from medium and long range is used to adjust group size and shape as well as to fine-tune arrow flight.

The methods and ideas in the next two chapters are the reason you bought this book. Keep in mind they are not a guarantee for success. Only your own consistent effort and patience can bring reliable performance from the bow-arrow-shooter system that you are going to build. The methods presented here offer the shortest possible route for achieving that reliability.

Tuning the bow for hunting begins with an understanding of the information in the previous chapters. The most important aspect is, of course, shooting the bow set at the proper draw length for you. After that has been established, the successful fine tuning of the bow and arrow system can begin.

To avoid complications later, the filled bow quiver and stabilizer should be added to the bow before tuning begins. Usually the quiver and stabilizer only change the point of impact of the arrow. Sometimes, however, the extra weight added to the bow handle will change the reaction the arrow has to the rest. To be sure this doesn't happen, place several arrows in the quiver and experiment with the quiver on and off the bow to determine whether there is any difference.

Fletch Clearance

The first phase of the fine tuning process for hunting bows is creating fletch clearance. Contact between fletching and arrow rest or with the sight window will cause each arrow to fly differently. Clearance, therefore, must precede every step in the tuning process except setting the draw length.

To obtain fletch clearance, you must examine one or more of six possible factors which contribute to fletch contact. These six factors are:

1) The nock rotation on the arrow;
2) The nocking point location on the string;
3) The tension of the cushion plunger or other side plate material of the rest;
4) The location of the parts of the arrow rest;
5) Arrow shaft sizes;
6) Fletching styles.

The last two factors are more or less last resorts.

Factual data can be obtained about the fletch contact by spraying white powder on the fletched end of the arrow. Many brands of white powder foot spray, which can be used for this purpose, can be found in a drugstore (Fig. 56). Once the fletching and nock end have been sprayed, shoot the arrow at close range. The powder on the arrow and fletching will be marked wherever contact with the arrow rest exists. Contact on the arrow shaft between the fletching is acceptable, but any contact the fletching has with the arrow rest is not acceptable.

In addition to spraying the arrow, you may want to spray the sight window area (Fig. 57). If the fletching is making contact with either the arrow rest or the sight window, some markings should appear on the white powder. In any event, the collection of facts is of primary importance before making adjustments.

Slight contact of the fletching with the arrow rest can be corrected by several adjustments. If the lower hen fletch is making contact, then raising the nocking point on the string can sometimes eliminate the

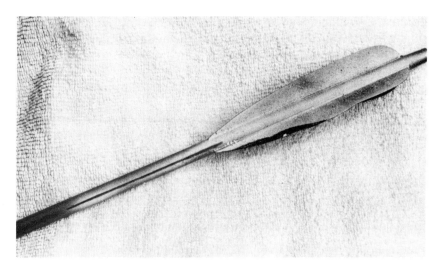

• Fig. 56. Spray white powder on the shaft and fletching to check for possible contact between the rest and fletching. **Contact between the rest and the fletching, as shown, should be avoided.**

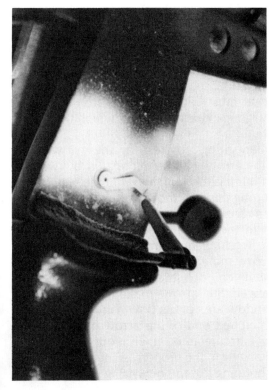

• Fig. 57. Spray powder on the sight window to be sure that no part of the arrow is hitting the handle riser.

contact. Usually this contact has to be corrected by rotating the nock on the arrow (Fig. 58). A slight rotation clockwise or counter-clockwise will position the bottom-inside fletch so it can pass the arrow rest without making contact.

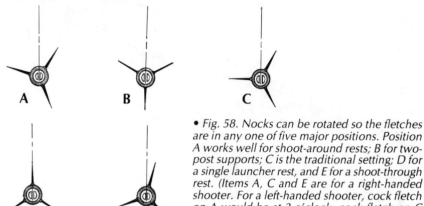

• Fig. 58. Nocks can be rotated so the fletches are in any one of five major positions. Position A works well for shoot-around rests; B for two-post supports; C is the traditional setting; D for a single launcher rest, and E for a shoot-through rest. (Items A, C and E are for a right-handed shooter. For a left-handed shooter, cock fletch on A would be at 2 o'clock, cock fletch on C would be at 3 o'clock, cock fletch on E would be at 4 o'clock.) Items B and D are the same for left- and right-handed shooters.

Sometimes all that is needed to eliminate the contact is an adjustment on the arrow rest. The shoot-through rest often is installed with the launcher too close to the cushion plunger or side plate (Fig. 59). This does not give the fletching space to pass through the arrow rest. In this case, the launcher must be moved away from the sight window and plunger so a larger gap exists through which the lower fletching can pass.

Fletch contact with a coiled-spring-type rest, or any rest with an extended support arm for the arrow, can be eliminated by two adjustments. The support arm often is too long and is in the way of the lower fletching (Fig. 60). Cutting this arm shorter often will eliminate a contact problem. I've often rebent the arm of the coiled-spring-type rest to eliminate contact with the fletch, as shown in Figure 61.

Severe contact between fletching and arrow rest may require changes in nock size and arrow spine. Nocks that do not fit the bowstring properly can cause the fletching to strike the arrow rest or sight window and should be changed. Stiff arrows make the fletched end of the arrow hit the sight window area of the bow handle, and weak arrow spine results in the fletched end of the arrow moving away from the sight window in an extreme amount. Either of these conditions can be corrected by changing to the properly spined arrow shaft.

Improper gripping and "bending" of the bowstring may cause ar-

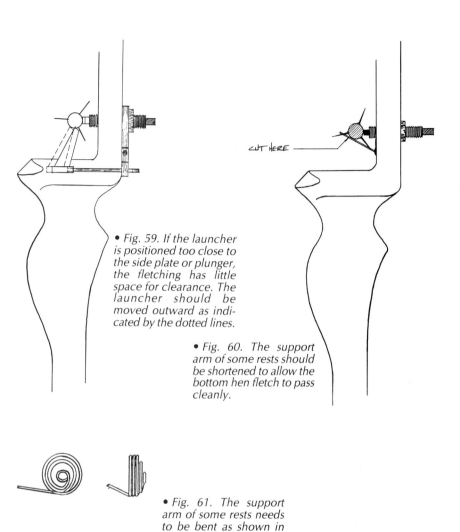

CUT HERE

• Fig. 59. If the launcher is positioned too close to the side plate or plunger, the fletching has little space for clearance. The launcher should be moved outward as indicated by the dotted lines.

• Fig. 60. The support arm of some rests should be shortened to allow the bottom hen fletch to pass cleanly.

• Fig. 61. The support arm of some rests needs to be bent as shown in the lower sketches so the top hen fletch passes the top of the rest.

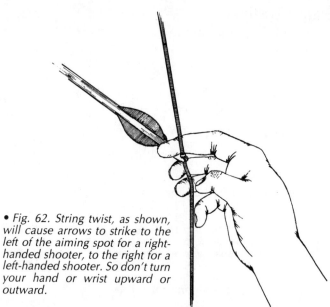

• *Fig. 62. String twist, as shown, will cause arrows to strike to the left of the aiming spot for a right-handed shooter, to the right for a left-handed shooter. So don't turn your hand or wrist upward or outward.*

row and fletching to strike the arrow rest (Fig. 62). Care must be taken to establish finger and wrist positions which allow the bowstring to keep its vertical alignment during the drawing of the bow and release of the arrow. Here's where a friend can spot the problem for you and help correct it. When the bowstring can be consistently held and released without the bending effect, then resume the fine tuning process.

Five-inch (or larger) full profile fletches and arrows with four fletches may make contact with the arrow rest which can never be eliminated. When the four-fletch orientation is 75 degrees/105 degrees (the most common), the fourth fletch on the arrow shaft means there will be less area between fletchings and a greater chance of contact when passing the arrow rest.

Large fletching will wrap around the shaft for a longer distance and will not pass the rest as easily as smaller fletching. Fletching that is installed with a helical curve will have difficulty passing around or through the rest without making contact. Regardless, **you should use helical fletching for broadhead shooting.** This means that a small amount of contact between rest and fletching may have to be tolerated as long as good flight and good groups are still possible.

Persistence in eliminating contact is a must for reliable performance. Contact must be checked on a continuing basis throughout the tuning process. A good bow tuner always is checking for contact, even when the arrows are grouping well.

Paper Testing

Phase two of the fine tuning process is the examination of short range arrow flight and the three basic adjustments needed to improve it. Improper nocking point placement on the string will cause the arrow to leave the bow in a nock-high position or a nock-low position. Arrow rest side plate tension which is not correct will cause the arrow to leave the bow with a fishtailing motion. When the arrow is not spined correctly for the bow-rest system, the nock end of the arrow will show a combination of these motions when shot. By adjusting for these conditions independently and in combination, you often can improve the flight of the arrow as it leaves the bow.

A simple square picture frame covered with newspaper is needed for testing short range arrow flight (Fig. 63). Start with the frame hung about four feet from the target. Stand two or three yards from the paper and shoot several fletched arrows through it. The holes will show the tears being made by the fletching as the arrow passes through the paper. When an arrow which passes the arrow rest cleanly is shot through the paper at close range, the hole in the paper is a record of the flight of the arrow. These holes can help you determine which adjustments are needed to achieve good arrow flight.

• *Fig. 63. A wooden frame covered with newspaper can be used to gather facts about short range arrow flight. Arrows shot through the paper from close range will make holes that show how the nock end of the arrow is flying relative to the point end.*

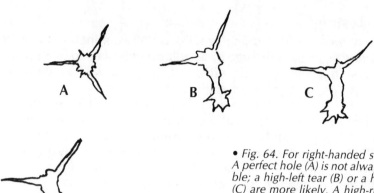

• Fig. 64. For right-handed shooters: A perfect hole (A) is not always possible; a high-left tear (B) or a high tear (C) are more likely. A high-right tear (D) or a tear to the right (E) should be avoided. Low tears should also be avoided. For a left-handed shooter, a high tear (C) or a high-right tear (D) are most desirable, and a high-left tear (B) or a tear to the left (just the opposite of E) should be avoided.

When the holes in the paper are not ideal, the first adjustment should be made to the nocking point location. If the fletching is tearing upward from the point of entry, the nocking point is too high and the nock-set on the bowstring should be moved downward. If the ripping of the fletching is downward, the nock-set should be moved upward on the string. Further testing will indicate when the nocking point is as good as it is going to get (Fig. 64).

This adjustment of the nocking point is not the final adjustment you will make. Later, when you shoot broadheads, you will want to experiment with other settings of the nocking point.

You may also want to experiment with nocking point when shoot-testing field points. The final setting of the nocking point is determined by which setting yields the best groups in the target.

The nocking point should consist of at least two Nok-Set rings placed together above the nock of the arrow. This will insure that the nocking point won't move after some use. Use a nocking square to set and check this important measurement on a regular basis.

Many times archers using a launcher-type arrow rest will experience nock-high tears when paper testing. This is often due to a launcher that is too stiff. A less stiff, longer or narrower launcher will help lessen the nock-high tears in the paper. When you begin shoot-testing from long range, minor adjustments to the launcher can be tested. A change in the stiffness — either stiffer or weaker — of the launcher can improve your long range groups.

The second adjustment indicated by paper testing involves right or left tears by the fletched end of the arrow. For right-handed shooters, fletching that tears to the left usually is the result of an arrow that is too weak in spine for the bow system. An arrow that tears to the right usually is too stiff. (The reverse is true for left-handed shooters.) Adjustments to the arrow rest can help eliminate the sideways motion of the arrow.

If an arrow is slightly weak in spine for the bow-rest system, the cushion plunger tension or side plate should be made stiffer. The stiffer side tension will cause the arrow to stay closer to the arrow rest as it passes the bow handle. Adjusting draw weight downward and moving the arrow rest away from the bow handle can also cause the arrow to pass the bow handle with less nock-left movement (right-handed shooter).

When the arrow is tearing to the right for a right-handed shooter, the arrow is acting stiff. To correct this situation, decrease the tension on the cushion plunger or side plate. The weaker side tension will cause the arrow to move further away from the bow handle as it passes the arrow rest. Also try increasing the draw weight of the bow to accommodate the stiffer arrow. The center alignment of the rest can be moved toward the bow handle so the point of the arrow is more in line with the direction the arrow is trying to fly.

The Easton chart for arrow weight and spine is a good reference to use when getting started in selecting the proper arrow for your draw weight and draw length. You should be able to find two or three arrow sizes which might work well for your system. Don't be afraid to try others as well. When the adjustments mentioned above do not obtain the desired results, try a different diameter or different wall-thickness arrow shaft. Remember that the final determining factor in choosing an arrow is the groups that end up in the target.

Learning to use the paper test can save hours of frustration. Knowing that you have good arrow flight before going to long range shooting can really boost your confidence, and this positive approach to tuning at long range will yield better results.

Shoot Testing With Field Points

The third and final phase of field point tuning is shoot-testing from medium and long range. Field points must group reasonably well before broadheads are shot. This will ensure that the bow system and the archer are both working consistently. Then and only then can you be certain that any problems arising are due to the effects of the broadhead and not your shooting fault.

Shooting at medium ranges (10 to 20 yards) and long ranges (30 to 60 yards), will give you an opportunity to make final adjustments to four parts of the bow system for best groups:

1) The peep sight, if you use one, needs to be set;
2) Sight pins need to be set;
3) Nocking point location needs to be set;
4) Cushion plunger tension needs to be set.

Begin shooting field points at 15 yards. This is the range where the peep sight can be adjusted and your anchor can be formed. The peep sight, if you use one, must allow you to be comfortable when anchored and aiming, and it must allow you to see through it in relatively low light conditions often encountered when hunting — so test it in low light conditions.

A bow drawn while your eyes are closed should have the peep in line with your aiming eye when you open that eye. Your anchor location must be comfortable and consistent shot after shot. The head position when using a peep should be erect throughout the shot. The anchor must be at the side of the face for this to happen. Since the anchor is unique to each shooter, it may take some time to develop.

When a peep sight is not used, the anchor should allow you to place your nose, lips or chin on the string. This will provide a consistent location for the anchor. A kisser button is very helpful here, as a rear sight locator, since it will put your head and aiming eye at the same location for every shot. Practice will bring the consistency desired. A simple test of nine shots can yield the first indication as to how well the bow is grouping. After setting a 15-yard sight pin, shoot three groups of three arrows each at a three-inch spot. The gold rings of a FITA international 40 centimeter target make a good objective at this distance. When shooting nine arrows at this three-inch spot, you should be able to hit the gold at least six times. Six hits out of nine shots will determine whether the bow is grouping or not. Repeat this test several times if you think you can do better on the second or third try.

Shooting at short range allows you to become accustomed to a new bow or to a bow which has had its draw length adjusted. When you cannot get comfortable with the bow at this range, the draw length should be adjusted until comfort is attained. Shooter comfort is essential to attaining consistency and reliability with the bow you plan to use for hunting. If you're comfortable with it, you will have confidence in it.

Failure of the bow system at 15 yards indicates a need for two courses of action:

1) Review your shooting skill level if it is not what it should be. Practice some more.

2) The other course of action is to adjust the bow system to make

it perform better. This involves moving the nocking point and redo-ing the nine-shot test. Repeat this test using several different nock locations until you are successful. Continued failure means retesting with each of several different plunger tensions. Further failures in-dicate a need to try other sizes of arrow shafts or a different draw length.

Once success is achieved at close range, shoot testing should be done at 40 or 50 yards. Long range shooting gives you a better look at arrow flight and a better picture of arrow groups. The nine-shot test at 40 yards should get a passing grade if six of nine shots hit a nine-inch spot. The blue, red and gold rings of the FITA 40 centimeter

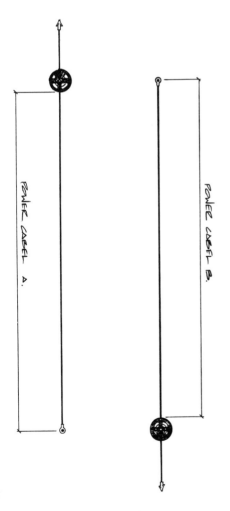

• Fig. 65. Both power cables on a compound bow must be the same length to obtain syn-chronized roll-over of both ec-centric wheels.

face are that size. Failure at this distance requires the same adjustments that were made at 15 yards and the same retest procedure.

When adjustments to nocking point and plunger tension do not yield good results an arrow of different spine must be tried. An arrow that is spined slightly incorrectly for your bow will be most evident at a longer range. Group testing with several different sizes of shafts should be done until the best shaft is found. At this time patience and repetition is a must. If field points don't fly and group well, then it is highly unlikely that broadheads will fly and group well.

Persistent flight problems require that you back up in the tuning process and recheck draw length and eccentric roll-over. When both eccentric wheels are not synchronized, the cables must be adjusted so the wheels roll together (Fig. 65). A slightly longer or shorter draw length should be tested to locate a better fit. Proper draw length and roll-over are the most important factors in creating good arrow flight with the compound bow.

Longbow and recurve shooters will have to do some experimenting with shafts that are of different spine to obtain good arrow flight. The arrow must bend the proper amount as it moves around the bow handle. Some padding may have to be added to or removed from the side plate or shelf of the arrow rest to help create good arrow flight.

The tuning process is not necessarily a short one. Sometimes it takes days working on a bow before you get acceptable results. Be patient.

Chapter 7

Broadhead Tuning And Shooting

The fine tuning process for broadhead-equipped arrows has four stages:

1) The first stage is the proper installation of the broadhead to insure true flight;

2) The second is testing for fletch clearance by using the powder test;

3) The optional third stage is checking the initial flight characteristics of the arrow by using the paper test;

4) Fourth and last, shoot testing at medium and long range is used to adjust arrow flight and grouping.

Hard work with field points will pay off when the broadhead is installed on your arrow. Field point shooting should have given you an opportunity to set the correct bow draw length and to determine the arrow that is properly spined for the bow system being used. This should make broadhead flight reasonably easy to attain.

There are exceptions, however. For that reason, the tuning steps for broadhead-equipped arrows must be taken with caution and thoroughness. Once again, exercise patience.

When broadhead blades are placed on the front of the arrow, they not only will uncover some existing problems that field points did not, they will cause some new problems. This means that shooting broadheads will not be the same as shooting field points. Many tuning steps have to be repeated to obtain the best possible results. With these thoughts firmly in mind, proceed with confidence and caution.

Installation

To minimize the effects of the blades being installed on the front of the arrow, take care to insure that the ferrule point of the broadhead is mounted in a straight line with the arrow shaft. This is the only way to be certain that each broadhead will be mounted the same and will have the same effect on the flight of the arrow.

As mentioned in Chapter Four, straightness of the point of the broadhead with the shaft is simple to check. Rolling the arrow on a narrow board or in an arrow straightener will reveal a point that is wobbling and not mounted properly. Take the time to install each broadhead so it is in line with the shaft before continuing the tuning stages which follow.

Powder Testing The Broadhead

The second stage of tuning your broadhead-equipped arrows is to check fletch clearance with the powder test. The powder test for broadheads is the same as it is for any other arrow. Spray the fletched end of the shaft as well as the fletching. Shoot the arrow into a solid broadhead backstop (Fig. 66). This will stop the arrow before the

• *Fig. 66. A dense-foam target butt is a good backstop for broadheads.*

powdered end gets to the target and will allow you to examine the sprayed portion of the arrow.

The marks on the fletching made by the arrow rest tell the story about contact between fletching and arrow rest. When there is contact on the leading edge or on the sides of any of the fletches, your arrows are not going to group consistently (Fig. 67). Marks on the arrow shaft will not cause any problems and indicate that the arrow is staying on the rest as it passes by the bow handle. Shaft contact is desirable, but fletch contact is not.

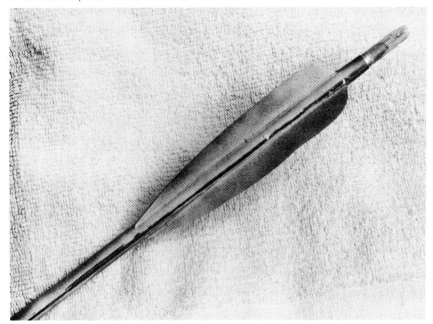

• Fig. 67. The fletching should not be marked by the arrow rest as the arrow is passing the bow handle. A contact mark on the shaft, made by the support arm or launcher, is acceptable.

Even if you powder tested your field points and found no contact, you must retest the broadhead-equipped arrow. Enough difference in flight characteristics can exist to cause the broadhead arrow to hit the rest. Don't fall for the old line which says ''broadheads that weigh the same as field points will shoot the same''. As mentioned earlier, this is not the case. Powder test and be sure.

Fletching contact with the handle riser of the bow will also affect arrow flight and groups. Spray the sight window area around the arrow rest to see if the fletching is hitting the side of the bow handle (Fig. 68). If it is, then the arrow rest will have to be moved away from the bow handle so the center of the arrow rests further from the sur-

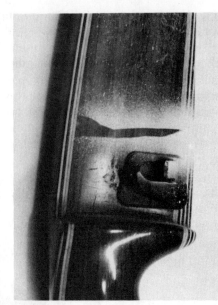

• Fig. 68. Fletch contact with the sight window should be avoided. Adjust the rest so the arrow is further from the handle riser.

• Fig. 69. Powder on the sight window will also indicate when the broadhead may be making contact on an over-draw setup, as shown here by the light horizontal line scratched through the raised area.

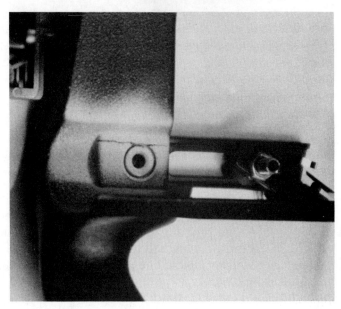

face of the sight window. This will give more space for the fletching to pass by the sight window. Another solution to the fletching contact problem would be to use weaker arrows.

As for contact on the fletching, the same corrections apply now as applied for field point testing in the previous chapter. Rotate nocks, change the nocking point, alter the arrow rest and try other arrow sizes until the desired results are obtained. Stay with this; it is important.

One additional item the powder test will reveal is contact between the broadhead and the sight window (Fig. 69). Bows equipped with an overdraw arrow rest should be checked for this kind of contact. If it occurs, you will probably hear it or feel it as you draw the bow to full draw. This problem should be cared for immediately. Heat the point insert so ferrule and the blades can be rotated; then they won't strike the bow handle. You also can move the arrow rest away from the sight window. Don't proceed until clearance is obtained.

Paper Testing The Broadhead

Paper testing broadheads is optional. If you elect to use it, field point testing rules apply. A perfect hole showing only fletch and blade slices through the paper is great if you can get it. But, usually you will have to settle for that ½-inch high-left tear (for right-handed shooters) or ½-inch straight high tear. These kinds of holes indicate that the broadhead and arrow are leaving the bow in a stable position.

I usually don't paper test my broadheads. This gets tricky when it comes to reading the holes in the paper and when setting up a paper frame in front of the broadhead target. But if I am having continuing difficulty tuning a bow, I will try it so I'm sure about what the arrow is doing as it leaves the bow.

Shoot-Testing The Broadhead

The fourth and final phase of the tuning process for broadheads is shoot-testing at medium and long range. By beginning at 15 yards and progressing to longer distances, you can gradually uncover and correct any flaw in the bow-arrow system. This way, equipment damage and frustration levels can be kept to a minimum.

Shooting broadheads should begin at 15 yards using three arrows shot at different aiming spots. The 15-yard sight pin you adjusted for field points or the point of aim you used previously should work well enough to keep your arrows on the target. You need several shots

● *Fig. 70. Test three broadheads by shooting at a three-spot target. This will indicate the consistency of your broadhead flight and groups.*

to get comfortable shooting the broadheads, so take a few before beginning the next step.

Don't expect your broadhead-equipped arrows to hit the same place as your field points — they may do so, but don't count on it. What you are looking for is some measure of consistency. Shooting three arrows at three different spot targets on the backstop should result in three arrows in the same relationship to the center of each spot (Fig. 70). If they don't all hit the same at the same relative location, then you need more practice or some bow tuning must be done to establish consistency.

Shooting three arrows at a time means you will have to use three sets of blades or three complete broadheads for practice. Make the sacrifice and do this right. A small investment at this stage of the tuning process is not much to ask considering the investment of money, time and effort you have already made. Besides, when three arrows with broadheads are grouping, you can be confident that any one of those with new blades will go where it is aimed when that big buck moves in front of you.

Broadhead Tuning and Shooting

Adjust your 15-yard sight pin so your arrows are hitting near the middle of the spot. Then shoot three ends of three arrows each. At 15 yards, your accuracy level should be six out of nine in a three-inch circle. No shots should be outside a six-inch circle.

Repeat this test several times if you feel it is necessary. If you think the three-inch circle is too small for your skill level, allow yourself a six-inch aiming spot.

If you do not have success with this test, make one of four adjustments:

1) When arrows tend to hit both left and right of the spot, change the stiffness of the cushion plunger and retest. Try two or three different settings before going further.

2) As the second adjustment, raise the nocking point. Test several settings.

3) If these adjustments have little effect, double check for fletch contact with the powder test.

4) If there is no contact, try increasing the draw weight of your bow and repeat the test.

At this point, continued failure requires testing several arrow sizes. Be patient; this is the right way to do it.

There are three adjustments which can be made for high and low arrows. Vertical groups in the target indicate that the arrow is leaving the bow with the nock end flipping high. Try three adjustments:

1) Try lowering the nocking point on the bowstring. Test several settings of the nocking point before going to the next adjustment.

2) You also can try a more flexible launcher if you are using a rest equipped with one. More flex in the launcher will allow the arrow to ride lower as it leaves the bow. Spring-coil-type arrow rests come in different weights with different numbers of coils. If this is the style you are using, try several different coils until good arrow flight is achieved.

3) Rests with rigid support arms under the arrow should be altered so the support has more vertical flex in an effort to eliminate the high-low groups in the target.

When none of these adjustments get good results, the problem may be in one of three areas:

1) Draw length and eccentric roll-over of the compound bow must be rechecked closely and reset if necessary.

2) Shooting form must be examined. An experienced archer could help you at this point by watching you shoot and discussing possible flaws in form that you might want to correct.

3) Last, if you skipped any steps in the tuning process, now is the time to go back to them so nothing is overlooked.

Long Range Shooting

Long range shoot-testing begins at 25 yards and progresses 10 yards per step until you reach a distance that is 10 yards farther than any hunting shot you plan to take. Don't skip any distances. Build your confidence a little at a time, and avoid getting frustrated. As you can see, this is not a procedure which can be done the night before opening day of the hunting season. June is a good month to get ready for October.

Begin at 25 yards and follow the same shooting procedure as used at 15 yards. Make six or eight shots to establish a good pin setting before making the nine-shot test. Your success rate should be six of nine arrows in a six-inch spot. No shots should be outside a nine-inch spot. If the target is too small, allow yourself another three inches diameter. Success here qualifies you for the 35-yard distance.

If your hits in the target are inconsistent, repeat the set of adjustments listed for the 15-yard distance. Don't forget to check arrow straightness and ferrule alignment with the shaft. Shooting into a firm backstop may cause bent arrows or loose ferrules. Double check the other parts of your system to be sure nothing is loose or out of alignment. This kind of check should be done on a regular basis with a hunting bow since it does get banged and bumped a lot.

The procedure for shoot testing at 35 yards is the same as at shorter distances.

Always shoot three arrows and work your way back to at least 10 yards farther than you intend to shoot at a game animal. For eastern whitetail deer, the desirable range is within 25 yards, so testing to 35 yards is recommended. Western hunting is done with longer shots in mind, so tuning and testing is more demanding. If 60 yards is your expected shooting distance, be sure your broadheads are grouping at 70 yards.

The 40 centimeter, multicolored FITA target face gives a specific spot size for each distance tested. The spot sizes are just about equal to the spot sizes given in inches in preceding paragraphs. At 15 yards use the gold ring, but at 25 yards add the red rings to the acceptable spot size. At 35 yards, use the gold, red and blue rings (nine inches) for your acceptable target. Add the black rings (12 inches) for shooting at 45 yards and the white rings (15 inches) for shooting at 55 yards. For longer distances, use all the rings just as you do for 55 yards.

My personal shooting standard at 60 yards is to hit the red and gold at least seven of nine shots, but I practice all year long and should be able to hit a target that size. If you cannot hit the entire 40 centimeter FITA target face beyond 55 yards, I recommend you confine your shooting to considerably less than 55 yards. Don't scare the game

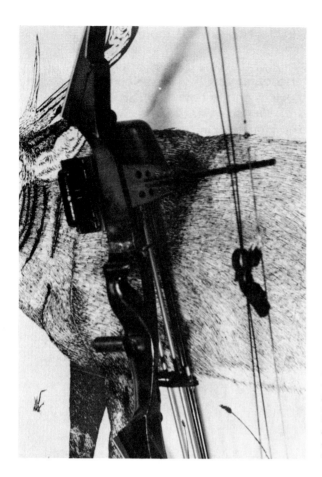

• *Fig. 71. This bow is fully equipped for the hunt. Daily one-shot practice sessions will be the final test before the bow is ready . . . and before your head and shooting form are ready.*

away or take the chance of a bad hit. You might get a better shot later in the day or tomorrow.

By using the adjustments on plunger tension, launcher tension, draw length and nocking point, the proper arrow for your bow can be made to group broadheads to acceptable standards. When you don't persist with these tuning techniques, you never can be sure where that first shot at a game animal will go, and that usually is the only shot you are going to get that day at that animal, and possibly the only one at any animal.

After you are certain your broadheads are grouping, prepare the same test arrows for your hunt. Replace the blades, or replace the entire broadhead if necessary, and use those test arrows for hunting. By doing this, you are eliminating the chance that a bad arrow is going to be used for that first shot. Then use your practice blades or practice broadheads to develop several more reliable arrows as needed.

Now is the time to mount the bow quiver, string tracker or any other aids you like to use for hunting (Fig. 71) if you haven't already done so. With these devices on the bow, you can set sight pins or determine the points of aim you want to use. Be sure to install everything you plan to have on the bow before setting sight pins, since these devices can change the point of impact for the arrow. The stabilizer you use, if you use one, and the filled bow quiver, should have been installed and tested at the beginning of the tuning process, since their weight will affect your bow's tuning and handling.

Chapter 8

Noise Reduction

As a rule, well tuned bows generate less noise, but this is not always the case. By having the proper draw length, the proper arrow size and the proper arrow rest adjustment, most noise problems will be corrected.

When noises persist, you need to examine seven possible sources — bowstring, arrow rest, limb mounts, quiver, fletching, sight and, on the compound bow, cables.

The importance of silence ought to be well understood by every bowhunter. The bow is a short-range hunting tool. We want high-percentage shots at UNALARMED animals; that won't always happen, but that's always what we strive for. At close range, three things are highly important:

1) undetectable or unalarming human odor;
2) undetectable or unalarming movement;
3) silence.

A well-tuned bow is understood to exist already. The three factors given here combine to produce effective camouflage.

The quarry shouldn't know or suspect that we are anywhere around.

If everything works the way it should, a fatally hit animal may not spook into wild flight or it may not react at all. We don't want wild flight, because that can lead to an impossible tracking and trailing situation, which obviously would reduce our chances of recovering the animal.

Cable Noise

There are four basic sources of cable noise. The most common is when two power cables hit each other. Another is a cable hitting a yoke button. A third is cable vibration caused by low tension levels on the string and cables. Last, the eccentric wheels may not be synchronized, causing cable slap and vibration.

Regardless of the tuning steps taken, some compound bow cables continue to make noise. These noises can be cables hitting each other during the forward movement of the bowstring with the shot or during the recoil of the bow after the arrow has left the string. In this case, a simple plastic cable saver or cable slide mounted between the cable guard and the cables can dampen the noise (Fig. 72).

If the yoke mount in the cable system is vibrating against the wheel or the limb, spacers must be added between the parts that are hitting each other and making the noise (Fig. 73). A last resort is to add a covering of felt to the cables so the noise is dampened or eliminated.

Most often, multiple draw length wheels which have the cables in the longest draw position are noisiest. This is due to less prebend in the limbs and less tension on the cables in the brace position. Switching to the next larger wheel and adjusting the cables into the shortest

• Fig. 72. The cable saver and cable hook can be used to silence vibrating cables.

Noise Reduction

• Fig. 73. Spacers can be used between the cable and wheel to prevent the cable from rubbing or slapping the wheel.

position will yield approximately the same draw length but less noise.

When the wheels of a compound bow are rolling over out of synchronization, they may make a noise. The correction here is to place the bow in a bow press or loosen the weight bolts until the wheels can be removed. Then adjust the power cables to they are the same length. Having the wheels rolling the same is not only vital to making the bow shoot well but is necessary for low noise levels.

Bowstring Noise

A bowstring which vibrates loudly is the most obvious source of noise. It is also one of the easiest to fix. Some spider-like, rubber-legged silencers or yarn strands, tied to the bowstring, will eliminate most of the vibration noise.

On the compound bow, the cable guard can be too close to the bowstring and cause the string to slap against it. In this case, the cable guard should be moved or bent out of the path of the string. Some powder spray on the cable guard will quickly indicate if the string is hitting the guard.

Recurves and longbows sometimes have noisy strings due to string slap. The slapping noise is caused when the string hits against the limb. Brush buttons can be installed near the ends of the string to stop the string slap and also prevent leaves and twigs from being

Noise Reduction

lodged between the limb and string. String noise can also be stopped by adding yarn strands or other string silencers.

Arrow Rest Noise

The noise an arrow makes as it is drawn across the arrow rest is certain to destroy a hunting trip if it is not silenced. Many rests on the market today have plastic covering which can be added to prevent drag noise created by the arrow (Fig. 74) as it is drawn across the arrow rest. This noise can be a light scraping (which sounds anything but light in the woods) or a thin, high pitched keening sound closely resembling one violin string screaming like crazy.

On wire horizontal support arms, heat-shrink tube from any electrical supply store can be used to prevent noise. On horizontal support arms which cannot accept a heat-shrink tube, a strip of adhesive-backed moleskin or adhesive bandage tape can be fastened.

Sometimes the side plate and/or the tip of the cushion plunger needs identical silencing. An arrow probably won't squeal as much from pressure on this part as from the support arm, but don't take the chance.

Any material will, sooner or later, develop a hard spot where the drawn arrow continually rubs it. Pay attention to this and replace the material as needed.

• Fig. 74. Shrink tube can be used on many arrow rests to prevent the noise of the arrow sliding on metal. Felt or suede with adhesive backing can be placed around the rest to prevent noise when the arrow falls off the rest.

Sometimes a simple cleaning of the arrow shafts and arrow rest parts is all that is needed. If you keep your arrow shafts clean, the silencing material on the arrow rest will function properly longer.

The area surrounding the arrow rest should be padded. If the arrow falls off the rest or is accidentally lifted off the rest against the sight window, the padding will absorb the noise. Leather with adhesive backing is available for this procedure. Felt is another good covering material. So is adhesive-backed moleskin.

Limb Mounts and Limb Rockers

Some compound bows have a distinct crack every time the bow is drawn or shot. Many times this is a noise caused by plastic half-round rockers which are mounted between the limb and the handle. The noise occurs when these rockers do not fit correctly, are

• *Fig. 75. Limbs and brackets that rub can be separated by paper or felt to prevent noise. A lubricant can be sprayed on rockers that make noise.*

Noise Reduction

loose or are broken. The bow has to be disassembled to solve this problem.

If the noise is more of a squeak than a crack, the rockers may be too dry. Some Tri-Flon spray lube will relieve the noise. It may take some time for the lube to soak into the dry area.

Sometimes the sides of the limb may be rubbing against the mounting bracket. A little sanding of the limb may be necessary to prevent this kind of noise. A piece of paper or tape placed between the limb and the bracket will also help quiet the noise (Fig. 75).

If the noise is more of a crack than a squeak, look for a loose or broken half-round rocker. Many of these rockers are made from plastic and will break with use over time. Disassemble the bow by removing the weight adjustment bolts and replace the broken part. You may need to return the limb to the factory for this work.

Quiver Silencing

The most common source of noise is the bow-mounted quiver. Arrows may vibrate inside the quiver hood, fletched ends may click and rattle, and the quiver may vibrate against the bow. All these conditions must be corrected if the noise is to be stopped.

The quiver mount may need to be bent or otherwise adjusted so none of its parts other than the mount bracket can possibly touch the bow, and no arrows in the quiver can touch the bow's lower limb or be close enough to vibrate against it upon the shot. This will insure that when the bow is shot no quiver parts or arrow parts will bounce against the bow (Fig. 76). Placing a rubber pad between the bow handle and the quiver mount also well help silence things, especially if a mounting screw should happen to work a bit loose.

Sometimes a longer quiver may be needed to solve the problem. A quiver that is too short, i.e., there isn't enough distance between the hood and the clip, leaves too much arrow length protruding below the clip to flex and rattle. **A too-short quiver causes more noise than is realized, so check yours.**

When the arrows are rattling inside the quiver, several adjustments may be necessary. First, be sure that the quiver hood is large enough. Next, be sure the foam in the hood which holds and covers the broadheads is dense enough and thick enough to hold the heads securely. If not, add enough foam to keep the broadheads from hitting each other and help keep them from vibrating loose.

One simple thing will greatly increase your silencing efforts and increase the effective life of the foam in the hood — push each broadhead into the foam in the same slits each time you clip arrows into the quiver, instead of pushing them in wherever they line up. Randomly punching the foam quickly cuts it to shreds and ruins its holding ability. Yes, this will take a few seconds more, but the results are worth it.

The arrow shaft holder slots may have to be tightened so the shafts do not vibrate loose. This can be done by screwing a small screw into the rubber on each side of each arrow slot. This will expand the clip and reduce the diameter of the arrow slot.

If the arrow shafts are just too small for the slots, you may have to make new holders out of plastic or rubber.

Sometimes the noise is the result of an overloaded quiver. Three arrows usually are sufficient for many hunts in the East, Midwest and South, unless you also carry a couple extra arrows for small game shooting. However, in the West and/or in rocky terrain, sometimes you can't carry enough arrows.

If you want or need to carry a lot of arrows, you can:

• Find the largest bow quiver you can which has adequate spacing between arrows;

• Select a bow quiver which has a clip larger than the hood, meaning that the clip is large enough to fan the fletched ends of the arrows, as opposed to having them parallel to each other their full length.

• Add an auxiliary quiver, such as a belt or back quiver.

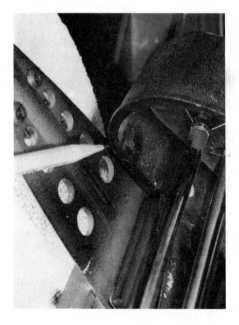

• Fig. 76. The quiver should not touch the bow except where the mount bracket(s) attaches to the handle. Be sure that the protective hood does not vibrate against the bow.

Fletching Noise

One disadvantage of using feathers is the noise they make. When five or six feathered arrows are placed in a bow quiver, sometimes it is difficult to keep them quiet. If they rub against one another or if they rub against your leg or a tree branch, the noise seems deafening in a quiet woods. Fewer arrows in the quiver or a cloth hood around the feathered ends may be a solution (Fig. 77).

A loaded quiver can be kept silent by carefully positioning each arrow so the fletches are positioned more or less parallel to each other instead of overlapping.

Sight Noise

Sight brackets and sight pins have a tendency to come loose and vibrate. The solution is to keep constant check on the mounting screws and the lock nuts on the pins. Lock washers sometimes can be added to prevent the nuts from coming loose (Fig. 78). Adhesive products can be added to the mounting bolts to keep them tight, and a rubber bushing between bow and bracket helps add a bit of tension to help keep screws tight.

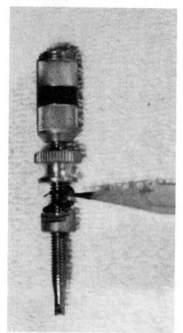

• Fig. 77. Slightly fanning the fletched ends of the arrows in a quiver will help keep the fletching silent. Best way to do this is to position the broadheads close together in the hood. Sometimes covering the feathers can prevent noise.

• Fig. 78. Sights, pins and sight brackets should be attached with lock washers so they do not vibrate loose. A drop or two of Loktite on the nuts may also work.

Noise Reduction

Chapter 9

Aiming And Shooting Strategies

First Shot Practice

Quality practice is a must if you are to achieve success in the field. Quality practice is an extension of bow and broadhead tuning. You might say it is the tuning of yourself for bowhunting.

Quality practice includes three important aspects:

1) Making the first shot count;

2) Practicing that first shot situation in all conceivable body positions and contortions, and in every sort of weather you intend to hunt in (or in simulated conditions, such as practicing with heavy mitts or gloves if you will hunt in cold weather).

3) Practicing enough, but not so much that your scouting efforts are inadequate or your efforts to learn as much as possible about the animal(s) you intend to hunt are inadequate. In other words, this is nothing more than recognizing ALL needs of your bowhunting efforts and getting each of them properly balanced in your planning and carrying out of those plans. They all are top priority items, but they must be balanced properly.

It boils down to this:

1) You can't hit the animal if you can't find it.

2) You seldom will have a high-percentage shot if you're a poor hunter.

3) You must know what is a high-percentage shot and what isn't.

4) You must never allow your shooting skills to become a crutch to help you compensate for lack of hunting skills or insufficient scouting time.

In most hunting situations you get one shot at the game animal you have been hunting. That one shot has to be good.

Since the first shot has to count, shoot as many "first shots" as possible. In preseason practice and then during the season when you practice, you should be focusing on the placement of the first shot you take. No warm-up shots and darned few "hold up there a second" shots are taken when you are hunting.

Each day before the season, and as much as possible during the season, you should be able to find three or four opportunities to pick up the bow and take one shot. Just one shot. This should be done with a broadhead-tipped arrow from 25 yards.

For instance, when you get up in the morning, get dressed, grab your bow, step outside and take one shot at the target — which should be a representation of the animal you will be hunting, just to help your mind and concentration. After breakfast and before going to work, take one shot. When you get home from work, take one shot. If you have a practice session in the evening, take one shot at the animal target, then go on to your regular practice.

Each of these "one shot" practice sessions is important in helping you develop a higher degree of concentration. You also learn whether you and your bow are tuned well enough to make that first shot count. When you can hit that first shot every time in practice, you gain confidence for those first shots on game in the field. Since you have practiced what you need to do in the hunting situation, you are ready for that part of your hunt — all other things being equal, of course. There is no moment of truth, no shoot-or-don't-shoot moment, with a target, but there sure is when a game animal is involved. And, of course, a target doesn't get the adrenaline rushing like the real thing does.

If you haven't done any "first shot" practice or if you are not very successful on a first shot basis, more practicing and maybe more tuning need to be done. Since you're ultimately part of the entire tuning process, it can be said that the tuning process is not completed until your first arrow is hitting the right spot.

If you are hitting only 50 percent of your first shots, you need to shoot more often and concentrate better. Your bow may need to be taken through the tuning steps again until any inconsistency is removed. You and your archery tackle need to be consistent. Pay your dues in front of the target instead of in front of that big buck, although you have to pay your dues in the woods, too. Nothing beats having been there. Practicing your shooting is a form of having been there as far as the shooting part of the entire sequence is concerned, but it still isn't the same.

• An empty one-gallon plastic milk jug, with a couple handfuls of sand for ballast, makes a good one-shot target. Have someone toss the jug, and you shoot at it wherever it lands. Obviously, this is best done from a tree stand, with the person doing the throwing in a safe position.

Varied Practice Shots and Positions

Practice on an animal target of the proper size so you groove your conscious and subconscious mind. This will help greatly in distance estimating. To a person accustomed to whitetail deer, the first sighting of an elk in the wild is mind boggling. The animal may be 60 yards away, but our mind says "Nah, the body that large must be only 35 yards, maybe 45."

Obviously, concentrate on a small aiming spot; don't look at the whole animal.

Practice shooting from distorted positions on the ground and from tree stands. You don't always get the classical shot position in the field. Sometimes you need to scrunch down to shoot between two spruce branches, for instance. Or that deer may come from a direc-

• A little in-camp practice, even if it is only from a picnic table instead of a tree stand, helps keep you in tune.

tion it was not supposed to, and you suddenly need to twist around the tree to shoot.

Shoot from trees so you'll become familiar with various foot positions and get practice shooting through holes in brush or over or under branches to learn the arrow's trajectory best. Sometimes, for instance, there will be an obstruction midway between you and the intended quarry. You may need to sight right through the obstruction, but the arrow's trajectory will take it over the obstruction, such as a log, and drop it into the vital area. But you won't know that unless you've practiced it.

Shooting from a tree stand in a tree will help you become accustomed to thinking about drawing elbow clearance, upper and lower bow limb tip clearance, the radius around your stand in which you can swing your bow and/or twist your body to get a shot. This also helps you become accustomed to judging distances from different elevations, to adjusting your shooting form (such as bending at the waist instead of dropping your bow arm) for shots at different elevations.

Practice from kneeling, crouching, standing straight, standing with body twisted right and twisted left, and from any other position you think may be handy to have practiced, so you know how your

94   Aiming and Shooting Strategies

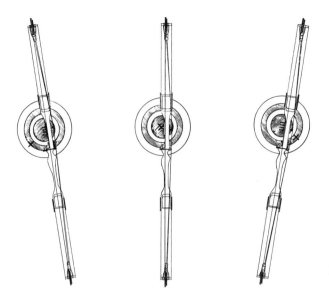

• Fig. 83. Canting the bow to the left will result in arrows hitting to the left and low, while canting the bow to the right will cause arrows to hit to the right and low.

shooting form changes or if it doesn't change from one position to another, whether you maintain the same draw length, etc.

It wouldn't hurt to practice with your bow canted at varying angles, as if you were trying to shoot under low-lying shrubbery or in a similar situation where for some reason or other you cannot hold your bow vertically.

Practice in early morning and late afternoon low light conditions; you'll see a fair amount of game under such conditions, and low light conditions affect your distance judging abilities.

Practice when it is misting or raining lightly so you will be accustomed to those conditions and know how your equipment performs under such conditions. Drawing on a nice deer is not the time to discover that a wet leather finger tab can develop a crease and cause the bowstring to hang up on release.

If you will wear a headnet when hunting, practice with one. You need to find out during practice if the eyeholes remain in proper alignment when you reach your anchor point, whether the fabric between your string fingers and your face affects your anchor point (mentally and/or physically), whether there's a chance any fabric can get caught on the bowstring before you release. In fact, practice with the clothes you'll wear when hunting. Hunting in cold weather means an extra layer or two of clothing. That clothing can affect your mobility and flexibility, your draw length, bowstring clearance, anchor, etc. Practice with the gloves or mitts you will wear when hunting.

Most bowhunters shoot a great deal before hunting season, but once hunting begins, few, if any, shots are taken. The reason is obvious — we have to spend time in the field if we are going to get a shot at whatever it is we are hunting. Despite the necessity of having to spend time in the field, we must put a little time into practice during the season if we intend to hit what we aim at. We can get rusty, our fine edge can dull, if we don't keep in tune.

Shooting From The Tree Stand

Shooting from the tree stand or any other elevated position requires aiming for a distance that is less than the actual distance between the shooter and the target. This compensation can be complicated by a lack of understanding about aiming at close range, such as zero to 10 yards. It is within this range that the arrow crosses from below the line of sight to above the line of sight, and the 10- or 15-yard sight pin **should not** be used for accurate aiming.

Shooting at a target, on level ground, which is closer than 10 yards requires an adjustment in your aiming strategies. Since the arrow is

• *Fig. 80. Don't miss any opportunity for a one-shot practice session.*

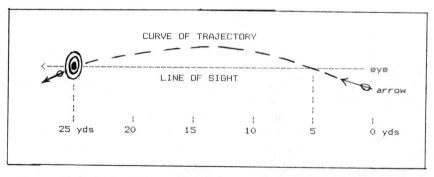

• *Fig. 81. Five yards can be hit by using the 25 yard pin, while a three yard target may require the use of the 35 yard pin . . . or gunbarreling may work just as easily.*

Aiming and Shooting Strategies

still below the line of sight before it gets to 10 yards, a sight pin that is lower on the sight bar must be used for aiming (Fig. 80). At five yards, you may need to use a pin that is set for 25 yards. Do some experimenting to find out exactly how you must aim your bow; it is not the same for every person and every bow.

Distances that are closer than five yards require a pin that is even lower. A target that is three yards away can be hit using a pin that is lower on the sight bar than the 25 yard pin. You may need to use a 35 yard pin to hit the target at three yards while someone else may use his 50 yard pin. Individual differences play a big role in close range shooting since no two people anchor, aim and release the same. Practice and experimentation are the only ways to find the correct aiming procedure for you.

There's one other aiming system you can use for the very close shot — gunbarreling. This can work for sight shooters and barebow shooters. It involves nothing other than shifting your anchor to just under your eye and looking right down the arrow shaft. With snap-on nocks, you even may want to place all three fingers under the nock so the arrow will be closer to your eye. At this close range, you certainly don't need to worry about trajectory, and you have a larger margin of error, so to speak, aiming at the vital region at three yards, for instance, than at 20 yards. This style of aiming takes practice, just as does everything else, but it can be effective, smooth and fast.

Any tree stand or downward angle shot of more than 15 yards is simple to calculate. Aim for the horizontal distance between you and

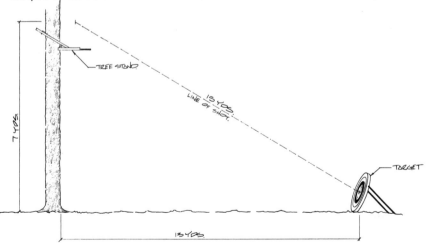

• *Fig. 82. The horizontal distance from your tree to the target is the distance which should be used for aiming. In this diagram, the hunter should aim approximately for 13 yards.*

the target and not the true distance between you and the target.

The horizontal distance is always less than the true distance to the downhill target. If a deer is 25 yards from your eyes and your eyes are seven yards above the ground, then the horizontal distance or aiming distance is 24 yards. If the deer moves to a position 15 yards from your eyes, then the distance from the base of your tree to the deer, the aiming distance, is 13 yards. When the deer is 10 yards from your eyes, then the aiming or horizontal distance is seven yards (Fig. 81). If the deer is eight yards from your eyes, aim for four yards.

If a deer is four yards from the base of your tree, do you know how to aim at it? Have you practiced aiming and shooting at four yards? What about one yard? Try it; it could be really important to you some day.

Another cause for our often shooting high from a tree stand is the different visual image of the animal target. We are accustomed to practicing from the ground, shooting at a broadside target which shows the target animal's body depth. However, a big game animal's body depth is greater than its body width, so when we view the animal from our position up a tree, we see more of the width than the depth. We also have a view which placed the spinal column more in the middle of the target than near the top. Since we're seeing more of the width than the depth, we're seeing a smaller image. Our brain says, "Less apparent inches visible, must be farther away. Aim for farther away."

The very next thought is "Now why did you do that? You didn't want to shoot high."

This high shot could have been a complete miss or a too-high-in-the-body hit.

This also is why we have to remind ourselves to aim low, low on such shots, lower than our subconscious and trained conscious wants us to shoot.

Shooting at an uphill angle is done the same as the downhill shooting and aiming. Shoot for the horizontal distance between you and the target. That means aiming as though it were a lesser distance. Practice will tell you which pins to use or the proper compensation when shooting barebow.

Sidehill Shooting

Any shot made along a hillside also requires some special aiming strategy. Without a level on the hunting sight, the shooter has a difficult time knowing when the bow is being held plumb or vertical. Aiming has to compensate for this problem.

Failure to hold the bow perpendicular to the horizontal will cause left and right shots (Fig. 82). Tilting or canting the top of the bow to the left will cause the arrow to shoot to the left. Similarly, if the top of the bow is canted to the right, the arrow will shoot to the right.

When a shot is taken on a hillside, it usually will result in an arrow that hits on the downhill side of the target. This is due to your not being able to hold the bow in a vertical plane. To correct this problem, you must aim slightly to the uphill side of the target or make a conscious effort to hold the bow in the vertical position. Either may be difficult to do in a hunting situation.

Some practice on sidehill targets and downhill targets will improve your performance with this difficult kind of shot.

Draw Length, The Bow And Angle Shots

Most shooters have a tendency to underdraw when aiming up or down hills. For compound bow shooters, this underdrawing can mean that the bow no longer is drawn into the valley. When the compound is not shot from the valley area of the force-draw curve, up and down angle shots cannot be completed consistently. The result can be an arrow that shoots erratically high. **From the tree stand, this can mean that a deer can be overshot even though the distance was judged correctly and you aimed correctly.**

Even when the draw length of the bow is adjusted correctly, care must be taken when drawing the bow for an uphill or downhill shot. If a conscious effort is not made to draw to your normal anchor point, inconsistent shooting will result. Practice from a tree stand will tell you if you and your bow need more tuning.

Sight Pin Strategy

Although there are many good sight pin arrangements which can be used for whitetail deer hunting, including a single movable pin, pendulum sights and range finder sights, my favorite is the fixed pin sight. The pins I use are set for 15 yards, 25 yards and for a longer range. The longest range pin usually gets set for 35 yards, but this varies depending on the speed of the bow I'm using.

The long range pin is set so the three pins on the sight can be used for a range finder. If the three pins are spaced correctly, the top or short range pin will be at or very near the top of the deer's back while the third and lowest pin will be at the belly of the deer when the deer is at 25 yards. When all three pins are on the deer, I start shooting. If the deer isn't close enough, I let it pass.

• *Steady now! Aim well, concentrate, release smoothly and follow through.*

Western hunting is a lot different. For the long range shooting that sometimes has to be done for elk, mule deer and other game, more pins have to be used along with a range finder. Sixty and 70 yard shots can be commonplace. This means bow tuning skills have to be developed so long range shots are more than a "by guess and by golly" operation.

• *A couple of approaches to a waterhole in these foothills was admirably covered from this tree stand. It meant sitting very still, but the self-control was worth it.*

Aiming and Shooting Strategies

Chapter 10

Tuning The Fast Flight Cable System

A) Introduction

The Fast Flight bow string has been on the market for several years and has made a significant contribution to archery. Its properties of light weight and high damping capabilities have increased arrow velocities and bow consistency. The high strength of this new string material allows it to be used on cam bows as well as on round wheel bows. It can be used as a bowstring and as a replacement for wire cables. Because Fast Flight helps to dampen the vibrations within the compound system, the noise levels of wheel bows and cam bows is reduced. It also resists cutting and fraying, which means it will take plenty of abuse on a hunting bow.

The material itself is high performance polyethylene. The developer, DSM of the Netherlands, engineered a process which arranges the polyethylene molecules so they are parallel. This feature of Dyneema SK60, the development name, gives it properties that can't be attained by any other method.

Dyneema SK60 has the greatest specific strength of any man-made fiber and is the only man-made fiber with low enough density to float on water. It is highly resistant to chemicals such as hydrochloric acid, gasoline and kerosene, as well as salt water and plain water. Dyneema SK60 combines the properties of high strength, low elongation, low weight and high durability. It has excellent resistance to light, resistance to abrasion, good flex life and great damping ability.

Jim Pickering, who has tested and developed Fast Flight systems for Hoyt, supplied me with technical information on Dyneema SK60. In tests he conducted, the cables and string withstood 1,500 dry firings on a 70-pound bow with no failure. After 300,000 cycles of a Fast Flight system, the only sign of wear was at the point where the two cables rubbed against each other, and this was minimal. At one hundred shots a day, this system would last for well over eight years with little or no wear.

One fault of Fast Flight is the slippery surface of the strands. This condition can allow the center serving to slide up the bowstring after some use. This, however, can be overcome by increasing the length of center serving above your nocking point to about three inches. The added length of serving will prevent the nocking point from moving.

When Fast Flight is used for the power cables on a compound bow, some changes occur:

• The high damping capability of this material will reduce the noise level of your bow.

• The omission of the tear-drop string anchor from the cable system is another change. Replacing cables is extremely easy since the Fast Flight system hooks onto an anchor pin on the wheel. Its most im-

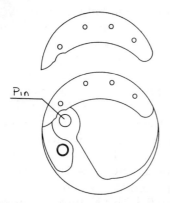
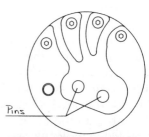

• *Fig. 84. This eccentric has two loop anchor pins on the bow string side of the wheel and one pin on the cable side. Changing either string or cable requires the use of some kind of bow press and can be done in three or four minutes.*

Tuning The Fast Flight Cable System

portant effect is the consistency it gives to the compound system.

As you continue to use this new style cable system, you realize that when twisting the cables to change their length you also control eccentric timing and draw length. One twist on one cable will have a small but noticeable effect on the eccentric timing and draw length. This change may be enough to improve your aiming of the bow and grouping of arrows shot from your bow.

Not all eccentric wheels are designed to receive a Fast Flight cable system. To use a cable made from Fast Flight, an anchor pin must be provided on the wheel (Fig. 84). The served loop on the end of the string cable is then hooked over the anchor. The string cable is then wrapped around the wheel, and its other end is attached to the axle of the other wheel. In some cases, the other end is attached to the yoke harness which is hooked to the axle. In either case, an anchor provision on the wheel is required.

B) Installation

The installation of a Fast Flight cable system involves two simple steps. First, the string cables must be the proper length and the needed servings must be in place. Next, the strings should be twisted to obtain the draw length you need and to set eccentric synchronization.

The length of the string cables should be about one-fourth inch shorter than the desired finished length. This will allow the tension of the limbs to bring the string to its shooting length. Remember, a Fast Flight string will only increase in length about 1/4 inch after installation. This is due to some stretching and slipping that takes place.

Care must be taken when building the Fast Flight cable system. I recommend using 18 or 20 strands in the cables. The end servings should be of braided Fast Flight serving thread, and should be long enough to extend around the wheel plus about two inches. The serving will help retard wear as the cable wraps and unwraps around the wheel with each shot.

After one end of the cable has been attached to the wheel, put 20 to 30 twists in the cable. This procedure will prevent minor frays on individual strands and increase the strength of the material. In fact, strength increases until the number of twists exceeds 100 per meter.

Before the cables are placed on the wheels, be sure to remove any burrs or sharp edges from the wheel. A small rat-tail file can be used for this purpose. This sequence of steps should be done while the bow is in a bow press and the wheels removed. Once all edges are smoothed, install the string cables on the wheels.

To prevent wear on the cables, it may be a good idea to use a plastic cable slide device on your cable guard. Most bows come equipped with this little item. The slide has two grooves which receive the cables and keep them from rubbing against the metal cable guard. I have used one on my own Fast Flight system for thousands of shots and have had only positive results.

Like the cables, the Fast Flight bow string must be made with care. A Number 18 center serving on 18 strands will make 1/4 or 9/32 inch nocks fit correctly. More strands or heavier serving will require the use of bigger nocks. The end servings of braided Fast Flight should be long enough to wrap completely around the wheel, while the center serving should extend about three inches above the nocking point.

When all cables and the bow string are in place, release the bow press slowly. Make sure that all strings are seating in the wheel groves as the limbs increase the tension of them.

At this point you are ready to begin tuning the eccentric wheel system.

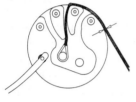

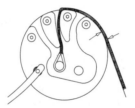

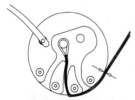

• Fig. 85A. At full draw, the bow string should be leaving both wheels at the same place in order to have synchronized roll-over and a smooth shooting bow. The timing marks (indicated by arrows on the wheels) indicate when, as in this drawing, the middle of the valley has been reached.

• Fig. 85B. When the bow is underdrawn, the eccentric wheels look like this drawing. The timing marks on the wheels have not rolled far enough to reach the middle of the valley.

• Fig. 85C. In this drawing, the timing marks have been drawn too far and have passed the middle of the valley.

• Fig. 86. The top wheel on this bow is rolling further than the bottom wheel, and neither wheel is in the middle of the valley. Add twists to the cable hooked to the top wheel or subtract twists from the bottom wheel cable.

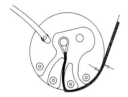

• Fig. 87. In this illustration, the bottom wheel is rolling further than the top wheel. Subtract twists from the cable hooked to the top wheel or add twists to the cable hooked to the bottom wheel.

C) Eccentric Wheel Synchronization

If the two Fast Flight cables are not the same length, twists must be added to or subtracted from one of the cables to balance the eccentric roll-over. One way of determining if the wheels are synchronized is to look at the position of each wheel relative to the limb. The limbs should cover the same part on both wheels. If not, an adjustment is necessary.

The best test for eccentric synchronization is to examine the wheels at full draw as shown in Figure 85. For this test, the bow string should be drawn in the center and not at the nocking point. In all probability your wheels will look like Fig. 86 or Fig. 87.

Figure 86 shows the top wheel rolling more than the bottom wheel, while Fig. 87 shows the bottom wheel rolling more than the top wheel. These conditions are easily corrected by twisting or untwisting the cables.

To adjust the eccentric positions in Fig. 86 you need only to add one or two twists to the cable attached to the anchor pin on the top wheel, or remove one or two twists on the cable attached to the bottom wheel. Adding twists to a cable will make it shorter which, in turn, increases draw length. Removing twists will, of course, make the cable longer and draw length shorter.

The wheels in Fig. 87 require the opposite adjustments. Add twists to the cable attached to the bottom wheel or untwist the top wheel cable. If the wheel balance is really bad, do a combination of both adjustments. Remember, the wheels will tell you when you are making the right adjustments and when you are not. Just check Fig. 85 to determine if your wheels are synchronized.

D) Adjusting Draw Length

After the wheels have been synchronized, adjust the draw length of the bow to match your draw length. There are four ways to do this:

1) twisting the bow string,
2) twisting both cables equally,
3) using different string anchor pins and string slots on the wheel and,
4) using a different size wheel.

Major adjustments to draw length are made by placing the bow string in different slots and hooking it to different pins. The rule to remember here: The more string between the two wheels, the more draw length you will have. The two drawings here show a wheel adjusted to the shortest position and to the longest position. The longest position lets as much string as possible out of the wheel so the length of string between the wheels is maximized. The shortest position pulls as much string into the wheel as possible and minimizes the length of string between the wheels.

It is important to note here that the string does not have to be positioned the same in both wheels. You may adjust one end of the string only. This adjustment changes the amount of string between the two wheels but does not change the eccentric synchronization. After each adjustment, check and reset the nocking point to its original setting because it will move up or down depending upon which end of the string is adjusted.

Changing the length of your bow string can also change the draw length. A longer bow string will increase draw length, while a shorter string will decrease draw length. A change of one-half inch in string length will yield about a 3/4 inch change in draw length. If such a change is not enough to match your draw length, and you have exhausted all the adjustments on the wheel, you should consider using a wheel of a different size.

Altering the length of both cables also will adjust draw length. Adding the same number of twists to each cable will shorten the cable but increase the draw length. Removing twists will shorten the draw length. Once the eccentrics are synchronized, the cables must always be twisted equally so synchronization is maintained.

• *Shortest Draw. The slots nearer to the limb tip will give the least amount of draw length. The pin that pulls more string into the interior of the wheel will give less draw length also. This illustration shows the shortest possible draw length available on this wheel.*

• *Longest Draw. The longest draw slot is the one farthest from the limp tip. The longest draw length available on this wheel is shown in this illustration.*

E) Tuning Procedure

After the Fast Flight cables have been adjusted and the string placed in the correct position for your draw length, your bow can be tuned the same as any other compound bow. Begin this by setting your nocking point on the string and powder testing the arrow for total fletch clearance.

During the test shooting phase of tuning, try different adjustments to your Fast Flight cables to improve the groups you are getting. One of the adjustments should be to add one or two twists to one of the power cables. By retesting for groups at 50 yards, you should see a difference. If groups and aiming are worse, try removing one or two twists. Try doing the same to the opposite cable. Collecting this kind of information will enable you to find the wheel balance which produces best arrow grouping for you and your bow.

Try adjustments to the draw length of the bow. This can be done in small increments by adding or subtracting an equal number of twists to each cable. Doing this systematically will help you find the draw length setting which allows you to shoot your best.

Tuning The Fast Flight Cable System

Chapter 11
Building And Tuning Arrows

A) Introduction

Once the bow is tuned, the next logical task in equipment preparation is arrow selection. Your choice of arrow involves the traditional aluminum tubular shaft versus the newer carbon tubular shaft. Both make excellent choices for hunting or target shooting if you follow the simple guidelines in this chapter.

If you intend to build your own arrows, use the procedure given later in this chapter. Read the procedure several times. Keep it handy when you begin building arrows. Skipping steps or rushing through any part of the procedure will give you less than the best results, so be thorough.

B) Size Selection

There is one very simple rule to follow when selecting the size of arrow you should shoot: **the size which flies and groups the best out of your bow while you are shooting it is the right size.**

This rule works all the time. Any other rule or chart or crystal ball will not give you the best all the time. Arrow size charts are certainly a source of good information, but don't think that they will give you the one, exact size for you and your bow. Charts are intended to give you a small group of sizes that should work well. Test shooting will be the final criterion for determining which size works best.

Printed in the next few pages are several manufacturers' size selection and comparison charts. When looking at them, you must select two, three or four sizes that are spined and weighted for your draw weight and let off. Borrow arrows of the apparent best sizes for you from members of your club or from a pro shop — if they will let you — and test them at both short and long ranges to determine which groups the best.

I know that not everyone is near a club or a pro shop. That makes it difficult to test several sizes before you buy. In such cases, select a size which favors the heavier weight and spine, whether it be carbon or aluminum. The heavier shaft is usually more stable, quieter and less prone to erratic flight. Speed is important, but remember that **a fast miss is still a miss and a noisy bow brings home no meat.**

Selection by Bow Weight/Arrow Length

The bow weight/arrow length chart should be read by first finding your peak bow weight in the left column, and then matching it to the vertical arrow length columns. For example, an archer using a 45 pound recurve with a 28″ shaft would likely shoot an Exacta 2100.

This chart is a guide for an 8% to 10% F.O.C. (Front of Center) balance point. If a shaft shoots too stiff, try a heavier point; if it shoots too weak, try a lighter point, or change the bow poundage and/or arrow length if possible. If these things fail to tune properly, try a different arrow size.

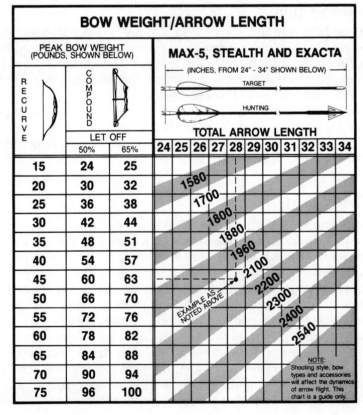

Selection by Shaft Comparison

Knowing what works for you now and finding an equivalent shaft on this chart usually provides the best results. Shafts which share the same level on the chart should shoot similarly if BALANCE POINTS ARE EQUAL. Equal balance points are obtained by using lighter points on comparably light shafts. AFC carbon arrow points are typically 10-20% lighter than points used on equivalent shooting aluminum arrows. If you switch from aluminum to AFC carbon arrows, and must keep the same point weight, you MAY need to select the next larger shaft than indicated on this chart.

Comparison of AFC and Easton aluminum shafts, weight in grains per inch at various shaft sizes

MAX-5™ Carbon	X 7 Aluminum	XX 75 Aluminum
— **1580** —		
— **1700** —	— **1516** —	— **1713** —
— **1800** —	— **1614** —	
— **1880** —	— **1714** —	
— **1960** —	— **1814** —	— **1816** —
	— **1914** —	— **1916** —
— **2100** —		
	— **2014** —	— **2016** —
— **2200** —		— **2114** —
	— **2115** —	— **2117** —
— **2300** —		
		— **2216** —
— **2400** —		— **2219** —
		— **2413** —
— **2540** —		
		— **2419** —

Determining **Correct Arrow Length**
Arrow length is measured from the bottom of the nock groove to the end of the shaft

For advanced target and field archers and clicker shooters, your **Correct Arrow Length** may be ½" to 1" shorter than your Draw Length.

Determining Draw Length
Length from bottom of the nock groove to the front side of the bow while at comfortable full draw

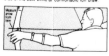

MAX-5, STEALTH & EXACTA		ALUMINUM SHAFT	
1580	*(4.42)	1413	*(5.92)
1580	(4.42)	1416	(7.15)
1700	(5.26)	1516	(7.34)
1700	(5.26)	1518	(8.45)
1700	(5.26)	**1614	(7.73)
1800	(5.84)	1614	(7.73)
1800	(5.84)	1616	(8.35)
1800	(5.84)	1618	(9.23)
1800	(5.84)	1713	(7.42)
1880	(6.38)	**1714	(8.06)
1880	(6.38)	1716	(9.03)
1880	(6.38)	1718	(9.99)
1960	(7.10)	**1814	(8.57)
1960	(7.10)	1815	(8.68)
1960	(7.10)	1816	(9.28)
1960	(7.10)	1818	(10.70)
1960	(7.10)	1913	(8.34)
2100	(7.89)	**1914	(9.28)
2100	(7.89)	1915	(9.18)
2100	(7.89)	1916	(10.05)
2100	(7.89)	1917	(10.71)
2100	(7.89)	1918	(11.58)
2200	(8.66)	**2014	(9.56)
2200	(8.66)	2016	(10.56)
2200	(8.66)	2018	(12.28)
2200	(8.66)	2020	(13.49)
2200	(8.66)	2114	(9.86)
2200	(8.66)	2115	(10.62)
2300	(9.50)	2115	(10.62)
2300	(9.50)	2117	(12.02)
2300	(9.50)	2216	(12.02)
2400	(10.36)	2216	(12.02)
2400	(10.36)	2217	(12.68)
2400	(10.36)	2219	(13.77)
2400	(10.36)	2317	(13.26)
2540	(11.57)	2419	(14.55)

*Number in parenthesis denotes shaft weight in grains per inch.
**Denotes X7 shafts, all others are XX75.

EASTON HUNTING

RECURVE BOW — Actual or Calculated Bow Weight (Pounds)					COMPOUND BOW — Actual or Calculated Peak Bow Weight (Pounds)				
Broadhead or Field Point Weight Only					Broadhead or Field Point Weight Only				
75 (GRAINS) 65-85	100 (GRAINS) 90-110	125 (GRAINS) 115-135	150 (GRAINS) 140-160	175 (GRAINS) 165-185	75 (GRAINS) 65-85	100 (GRAINS) 90-110	125 (GRAINS) 115-135	150 (GRAINS) 140-160	175 (GRAINS) 165-185
30-34	27-31	24-28	21-25	18-22	35-40	32-37	29-34	26-31	23-28
35-39	32-36	29-33	26-30	23-27	41-46	38-43	35-40	32-37	29-34
40-44	37-41	34-38	31-35	28-32	47-52	44-49	41-46	38-43	35-40
45-49	42-46	39-43	36-40	33-37	53-58	50-55	47-52	44-49	41-46
50-54	47-51	44-48	41-45	38-42	59-64	56-61	53-58	50-55	47-52
55-59	52-56	49-53	46-50	43-47	65-70	62-67	59-64	56-61	53-58
60-64	57-61	54-58	51-55	48-52	71-76	68-73	65-70	62-67	59-64
65-69	62-66	59-63	56-60	53-57	77-82	74-79	71-76	68-73	65-70
70-74	67-71	64-68	61-65	58-62	83-88	80-85	77-82	74-79	71-76
75-79	72-76	69-73	66-70	63-67	89-94	86-91	83-88	80-85	77-82
80-84	77-81	74-78	71-75	68-72	95-100	92-97	89-94	86-91	83-88

> This shaft selection chart was set up using Fast Flite® String, finger release and modern, efficient recurve and compound bows. The shaft size recommendations for compound bows were determined using 40-65% let-off and round wheels. If your equipment varies from the above, see the EASTON BOWHUNTING brochure to determine your **Calculated Bow Weight** or **Calculated Peak Bow Weight** before using this chart.

Shaft selection (Shaft Size · Shaft Model · Shaft Weight)

Column groups: 22" (21½"–22½") · 23" (22½"–23½") · 24" (23½"–24½") · 25" (24½"–25½")

Bow wt band (recurve 75-col)	22"	23"	24"	25"
30-34				1813 XX75 197 A
35-39			1913 XX75 209 A	1813 XX75 189 A · 1816 XX75,E 232 A · 3L-04 A/C/C 173
40-44		1813 XX75 181 A	1913 XX75 200 A · 1816 XX75,E 223 A · 1818 XX75 268 A · 3L-04 A/C/C 167	1813 XX75 209 B · 1816 XX75,E 232 B · 3-04 A/C/C 180
45-49	1813 XX75 173 A	1913 XX75 192 A · 1816 XX75,E 213 A · 3L-04 A/C/C 160	1816 XX75,E 223 B · 1818 XX75 257 A · 3-04 A/C/C 173	1916 XX75,E 251 A · 1818 XX75 268 B · 3L-18 A/C/C 186
50-54	1913 XX75 184 A · 1816 XX75,E 204 A · 3L-04 A/C/C 153	1913 XX75 192 B · 1816 XX75,E 213 B · 1818 XX75 246 A · 3-04 A/C/C 166	2013 XX75 216 A · 1916 XX75,E 241 A · 1818 XX75 257 B · 3L-18 A/C/C 179 · 3-18 195	2013 XX75 225 B · 1916 XX75,E 251 B · 3L-18 A/C/C 186 · 3-18 195
55-59	1913 XX75 184 B · 1816 XX75,E 204 B · 1818 XX75 235 A · 3-04 A/C/C 158	2013 XX75 216 B · 1916 XX75,E 231 A · 1918 XX75 246 B · 3L-18 A/C/C 179 · 3-18 187	2013 XX75 216 B · 1916 XX75,E 241 B · 1918 XX75 278 A · 3L-18 A/C/C 179 · 3-18 187	2013 XX75 233 A · 2016 XX75 264 A · 1918 XX75 290 A · 3-18 A/C/C 195
60-64	1916 XX75,E 221 A · 1818 XX75 235 B · 3L-18 A/C/C 164 · 3-18 180	2013 XX75 297 B · 1916 XX75,E 231 B · 2016 XX75 253 A · 1918 XX75 278 B · 3-18 A/C/C 187	2016 XX75 253 A · 1918 XX75 278 B · 2018 XX75,E 307 A · 3-30 A/C/H 202	2013 XX75 233 B · 2016 XX75 264 C · 2115 XX75 269 A · 2018 XX75,E 307 A · 3-30 A/C/H 202
65-69	2013 XX75 198 B · 1916 XX75,E 221 B · 1918 XX75 255 A · 3L-18 A/C/C 164 · 3-18 172	2113 XX75 214 A · 2016 XX75 243 A · 1918 XX75 255 B · 3-18 A/C/H 180	2113 XX75 237 B · 2016 XX75 253 C · 2115 XX75 259 A · 2018 XX75,E 295 A · 3-30 A/C/H 194	2213 XX75 246 A · 2114 XX75 227 C · 2115 XX75 269 B · 2018 XX75,E 307 B · 2020 XX75 337 B · 3-30 A/C/H 202
70-74	2113 XX75 205 A · 2016 XX75 232 A · 1918 XX75 255 B · 3-18 A/C/H 172	2113 XX75 214 C · 2016 XX75 243 C · 2115 XX75 259 B · 2018 XX75,E 282 A · 3-30 A/C/H 186	2213 XX75 236 A · 2115 XX75 259 B · 2020 XX75 324 A · 3-30 A/C/H 194	2312 XX75 239 A · 2215 XX75 267 A · 2020 XX75 301 A · 3-39 A/C/H 210 · 4-18 A/C/H 226
75-79	2113 XX75 205 C · 2114 XX75 217 B · 2016 XX75 232 C · 2115 XX75 237 A · 2018 XX75,E 270 A · 3-30 A/C/H 178	2213 XX75 226 A · 2115 XX75 248 B · 2018 XX75 282 B · 2020 XX75 310 A · 3-30 A/C/H 193	2312 XX75 225 A · 2215 XX75 256 A · 2117 XX75,E 282 B · 2020 XX75 324 B · 3-39 A/C/C 202 · 4-18 A/C/H 217	2312 XX75 235 B · 2314 XX75 266 A · 2215 XX75 267 B · 2216 XX75 301 A · 3-39 A/C/C 217 · 4-28 A/C/H 217
80-84	2213 XX75 216 A · 2114 XX75 217 C · 2115 XX75 237 B · 2020 XX75 297 A · 3-30 A/C/H 178	2312 XX75 216 A · 2213 XX75 227 B · 2215 XX75 245 A · 2117 XX75,E 277 A · 2020 XX75 310 B · 3-39 A/C/C 193 · 4-18 A/C/H 208	2312 XX75 225 B · 2314 XX75 255 A · 2215 XX75 256 B · 2117 XX75,E 289 B · 3-49 A/C/C 208 · 4-28 A/C/H 223	2413 XX75 260 A · 2314 XX75 266 B · 2315 XX75 292 A · 2216 XX75 289 B · 3-49 A/C/C 216 · 4-28 A/C/H 232

The chart indicates that more than one shaft size may shoot well from your bow. **Shaft sizes in bold type are the most widely used**, but you may decide to shoot a lighter shaft for speed, or a heavier shaft for greater penetration and durability. Also, large variations in bow efficiency, type of wheels or cams, bow length, string material and release type may require special bow tuning or a shaft size change to accommodate these variations.

The "Shaft Weight" column—indicates shaft weight only. To determine total arrow weight, add the weight of the shaft, point or broadhead, RPS insert, nock and fletching. Where two models are shown for one size, the weight shown is for XX75. Letter codes A-C listed to the right of shaft weight indicate the relative stiffness of each aluminum shaft within that "Shaft Size" box ("A" being the stiffest, "B" less stiff, etc.)

"Shaft Model" column—designates arrow model
XX75 = Gamegetter, Gamegetter II, Camo Hunter, Autumn Hunter and PermaGraphic shafts
E = Eagle Hunter shafts
A/C/H = Aluminum/Carbon/Hunter shafts
A/C/C = Aluminum/Carbon/Comp shafts

Determining **Actual Bow Weight** or **Actual Peak Bow Weight**

Actual Bow Weight of a recurve bow and **Actual Peak Bow Weight** of a compound bow can be determined at your archery pro shop.

Although Easton has attempted to consider most variations of equipment, there are other style and equipment variables that could require shaft sizes other than the ones suggested. In these cases, you'll need to experiment and use stiffer of weaker spine shafts to fit your situation.

See page 111 to determine correct arrow length and draw length

See page 111 to determine correct arrow length and draw length

SHAFT SELECTION CHART

25½"- 26" -26½"			26½"- 27" -27½"			27½"- 28" -28½"			28½"- 29" -29½"		
Shaft Size	Shaft Model	Shaft Weight	Shaft Size	Shaft Model	Shaft Weight	Shaft Size	Shaft Model	Shaft Weight	Shaft Size	Shaft Model	Shaft Weight
1913 **1816** 3L-04	XX75 **XX75,E** A/C/C	217 A **241 A** 180	**1913** **1816** 1818 3-04	**XX75** **XX75,E** XX75 A/C/C	**225 B** **251 B** 289 A 194	2013 **1916** 1818 3L-18	XX75 **XX75,E** XX75 A/C/C	252 A **281 A** 300 B 209	**2013** **1916** 1918 3L-18 3-18	**XX75** **XX75,E** XX75 A/C/C A/C/C	**261 B** **292 B** 336 A 216 226
1913 **1816** 1818 3-04	**XX75** **XX75,E** XX75 A/C/C	**217 B** **241 B** 278 A 187	2013 **1916** 1818 3L-18	XX75 **XX75,E** XX75 A/C/C	243 A **271 A** 289 B 201	**2013** **1916** 1918 3L-18 3-18	**XX75** **XX75,E** XX75 A/C/C A/C/C	**252 B** **281 B** 324 A 209 219	2113 **2016** 1918 3-18	XX75 **XX75** XX75 A/C/C	270 A **306 A** 336 B 226
2013 **1916** 1818 3L-18	XX75 **XX75,E** XX75 A/C/C	234 A **261 A** 278 B 194	**2013** **1916** 1918 3L-18 3-18	**XX75** **XX75,E** XX75 A/C/C A/C/C	**243 B** **271 B** 313 A 201 211	2113 **2016** 1918 3-18	XX75 **XX75** XX75 A/C/C	260 A **296 A** 324 B 219	2113 **2114** 2016 2115 **2018** 3-30	XX75 **XX75** XX75 XX75 **XX75,E** A/C/H	270 C **286 B** 306 C 312 A **356 A** 235
2013 **1916** 1918 3L-18 3-18	**XX75** **XX75,E** XX75 A/C/C A/C/C	**234 B** **261 B** 301 A 194 203	2113 **2016** 1918 3-18	XX75 **XX75** XX75 A/C/C	251 A **285 A** 313 B 211	2113 **2114** 2016 2115 **2018** 3-30	XX75 **XX75** XX75 XX75 **XX75,E** A/C/H	260 C **276 B** 296 C 302 A **344 A** 227	**2213** 2114 2115 **2018** 2020 3-30	**XX75** XX75 XX75 **XX75,E** XX75 A/C/H	**285 A** 286 C 312 B **356 B** 391 A 235
2113 **2016** 1918 3-18	XX75 **XX75** XX75 A/C/C	242 A **275 A** 301 B 203	2113 **2114** 2016 2115 **2018** 3-30	XX75 **XX75** XX75 XX75 **XX75,E** A/C/H	251 C **266 B** 285 C 291 A **332 A** 219	**2213** 2114 2115 **2018** 2020 3-30	**XX75** XX75 XX75 **XX75,E** XX75 A/C/H	**275 A** 276 C 302 B **344 B** 378 A 227	2312 2213 **2215** **2117** 2020 3-39 4-18	XX75 XX75 **XX75** **XX75,E** XX75 A/C/C A/C/H	272 A 285 B **309 A** **349 A** 391 B 244 262
2113 **2114** 2016 2115 **2018** 3-30	XX75 **XX75** XX75 XX75 **XX75,E** A/C/H	242 C **256 B** 275 C 280 A **319 A** 210	**2213** 2114 2115 **2018** 2020 3-30	**XX75** XX75 XX75 **XX75,E** XX75 A/C/H	**265 A** 266 C 291 B **332 B** 364 A 219	2312 2213 **2215** **2117** 2020 3-39 4-18	XX75 XX75 **XX75** **XX75,E** XX75 A/C/C A/C/H	263 A 275 B **299 A** **337 A** 378 B 235 253	2312 **2314** 2215 2117 **2216** 3-49 4-28	XX75 **XX75** XX75 XX75,E **XX75** A/C/C A/C/H	272 B **309 A** 309 B 349 B **349 A** 251 269
2213 2114 2115 **2018** 2020 3-30	**XX75** XX75 XX75 **XX75,E** XX75 A/C/H	**256 A** 256 C 280 B **319 B** 351 A 210	2312 2213 **2215** **2117** 2020 3-39 4-18	XX75 XX75 **XX75** **XX75,E** XX75 A/C/C A/C/H	254 A 265 B **288 A** **325 A** 364 B 227 244	2312 **2314** 2215 2117 **2216** 3-49 4-28	XX75 **XX75** XX75 XX75,E **XX75** A/C/C A/C/H	263 B **298 A** 299 B 337 B **337 A** 242 260	**2413** 2314 **2315** 2216 2219 3-49 4-28	**XX75** XX75 **XX75** XX75 XX75,E A/C/C A/C/H	**302 A** 309 B **338 A** 349 B 399 A 251 269
2312 2213 **2215** **2117** 2020 3-39 4-18	XX75 XX75 **XX75** **XX75,E** XX75 A/C/C A/C/H	244 A 256 B **277 A** **313 A** 351 B 219 235	2312 **2314** 2215 2117 **2216** 3-49 4-28	XX75 **XX75** XX75 XX75,E **XX75** A/C/C A/C/H	254 B **287 A** 288 B 325 B **325 A** 234 250	**2413** 2314 **2315** 2216 2219 3-49 4-28	**XX75** XX75 **XX75** XX75 XX75,E A/C/C A/C/H	**291 A** 298 B **327 A** 337 B 386 A 242 260	2512 2413 **2315** **2219** 3-60 4-39	XX75 XX75 **XX75** **XX75,E** A/C/C A/C/H	295 A 302 B **338 B** **399 B** 268 283
2312 **2314** 2215 2117 **2216** 3-49 4-28	XX75 **XX75** XX75 XX75,E **XX75** A/C/C A/C/H	244 B **277 A** 277 B 313 B **313 A** 225 241	**2413** 2314 **2315** 2216 2219 3-49 4-28	**XX75** XX75 **XX75** XX75 XX75,E A/C/C A/C/H	**281 A** 287 B **315 A** 325 B 372 A 234 250	2512 2413 **2315** **2219** 3-60 4-39	XX75 XX75 **XX75** **XX75,E** A/C/C A/C/H	285 A 291 B **327 B** **386 B** 259 273	2512 2315 **2317** 2219 3-60 4-39	XX75 XX75 **XX75** XX75,E A/C/C A/C/H	295 A 338 B **385 A** 399 B 268 283
2413 2314 **2315** 2216 2219 3-49 4-28	**XX75** XX75 **XX75** XX75 XX75,E A/C/C A/C/H	**270 A** 277 B **303 A** 313 B 358 A 225 241	2512 2413 **2315** **2219** 3-60 4-39	XX75 XX75 **XX75** **XX75,E** A/C/C A/C/H	275 A 281 B **315 B** **372 B** 250 264	2512 2315 **2317** 2219 3-60 4-39	XX75 XX75 **XX75** XX75,E A/C/C A/C/H	285 A 327 B **371 A** 386 B 259 273	2512 **2514** **2317** 3-71 4-49	XX75 **XX75** **XX75** A/C/C A/C/H	295 B **329 A** **385 B** 283 298
2512 2413 **2315** **2219** 3-60 4-39	XX75 XX75 **XX75** **XX75,E** A/C/C A/C/H	265 A 270 B **303 B** **358 B** 240 254	2512 2315 **2317** 2219 3-60 4-39	XX75 XX75 **XX75** XX75,E A/C/C A/C/H	275 A 315 B **358 A** 372 B 250 264	2512 **2514** **2317** 3-71 4-49	XX75 **XX75** **XX75** A/C/C A/C/H	285 B **317 A** **371 B** 273 288	**2514** **2317** 2419 3-71 4-49	**XX75** **XX75** XX75 A/C/C A/C/H	**329 B** **385 C** 422 A 283 298

29½"- 30" -30½"			30½"- 31" -31½"			31½"- 32" -32½"			32½"- 33" -33½"		
Shaft Size	Shaft Model	Shaft Weight	Shaft Size	Shaft Model	Shaft Weight	Shaft Size	Shaft Model	Shaft Weight	Shaft Size	Shaft Model	Shaft Weight
2113 **2016** 1918 3-18	XX75 **XX75** XX75 A/C/C	279 A **317 A** 347 B 234	2113 **2114** 2016 2115 **2018** 3-30	XX75 **XX75** XX75 XX75 **XX75,E** A/C/H	288 C **306 B** 327 C 334 A **381 A** 251	**2213** 2114 2115 **2018** 2020 3-30	**XX75** XX75 XX75 **XX75,E** XX75 A/C/H	**315 A** 316 C 345 B **393 B** 432 A 259	2312 2213 **2215** **2117** 3-39 4-18	XX75 XX75 **XX75** **XX75,E** A/C/C A/C/H	310 A 324 B **352 A** **397 A** 277 298
2113 **2114** 2016 2115 **2018** 3-30	XX75 **XX75** XX75 XX75 **XX75,E** A/C/H	279 C **296 B** 317 C 323 A **368 A** 243	**2213** 2114 2115 **2018** 2020 3-30	**XX75** XX75 XX75 **XX75,E** XX75 A/C/H	**305 A** 306 C 334 B **381 B** 418 A 251	2312 2213 **2215** **2117** 2020 3-39 4-18	XX75 XX75 **XX75** **XX75,E** XX75 A/C/C A/C/H	301 A 315 B **341 A** **385 A** 432 B 269 289	2312 **2314** 2215 2117 **2216** 3-49 4-28	XX75 **XX75** XX75 XX75,E **XX75** A/C/C A/C/H	310 B **351 A** 352 B 397 B **397 A** 286 306
2213 2114 2115 **2018** 2020 3-30	**XX75** XX75 XX75 **XX75,E** XX75 A/C/H	**295 A** 296 C 323 B **368 B** 405 A 243	2312 2213 **2215** **2117** 2020 3-39 4-18	XX75 XX75 **XX75** **XX75,E** XX75 A/C/C A/C/H	291 A 305 B **331 A** **373 A** 418 B 261 280	2312 **2314** 2215 2117 **2216** 3-49 4-28	XX75 **XX75** XX75 XX75,E **XX75** A/C/C A/C/H	301 B **341 A** 341 B 385 B **385 A** 277 297	**2413** 2314 **2315** 2216 2219 3-49 4-28	**XX75** XX75 **XX75** XX75 XX75,E A/C/C A/C/H	**343 A** 351 B **385 A** 397 B 454 A 286 306
2312 2213 **2215** **2117** 2020 3-39 4-18	XX75 XX75 **XX75** **XX75,E** XX75 A/C/C A/C/H	282 A 295 B **320 A** **361 A** 405 B 252 271	2312 **2314** 2215 2117 **2216** 3-49 4-28	XX75 **XX75** XX75 XX75,E **XX75** A/C/C A/C/H	291 B **330 A** 331 B 373 B **373 A** 268 288	**2413** 2314 **2315** 2216 2219 3-49 4-28	**XX75** XX75 **XX75** XX75 XX75,E A/C/C A/C/H	**333 A** 341 B **373 A** 385 B 441 A 277 297	2512 2413 **2315** **2219** 3-60 4-39	XX75 XX75 **XX75** **XX75,E** A/C/C A/C/H	336 A 343 B **385 B** **454 B** 305 322
2312 **2314** 2215 2117 **2216** 3-49 4-28	XX75 **XX75** XX75 XX75,E **XX75** A/C/C A/C/H	282 B **319 A** 320 B 361 B **361 A** 260 278	**2413** 2314 **2315** 2216 2219 3-49 4-28	**XX75** XX75 **XX75** XX75 XX75,E A/C/C A/C/H	**322 A** 330 B **362 A** 373 B 427 A 268 288	2512 2413 **2315** **2219** 3-60 4-39	XX75 XX75 **XX75** **XX75,E** A/C/C A/C/H	326 A 333 B **373 B** **441 B** 296 312	2512 2315 **2317** 2219 3-60 4-39	XX75 XX75 **XX75** XX75,E A/C/C A/C/H	336 A 385 B **438 A** 454 B 305 322
2413 2314 **2315** 2216 2219 3-49 4-28	**XX75** XX75 **XX75** XX75 XX75,E A/C/C A/C/H	**312 A** 319 B **350 A** 361 B 413 A 260 278	2512 2413 **2315** **2219** 3-60 4-39	XX75 XX75 **XX75** **XX75,E** A/C/C A/C/H	316 A 322 B **362 B** **427 B** 287 303	2512 2315 **2317** 2219 3-60 4-39	XX75 XX75 **XX75** XX75,E A/C/C A/C/H	326 A 373 B **424 A** 441 B 296 312	2512 **2514** **2317** 3-71 4-49	XX75 **XX75** **XX75** A/C/C A/C/H	336 B **374 A** **438 B** 322 339
2512 2413 **2315** **2219** 3-60 4-39	XX75 XX75 **XX75** **XX75,E** A/C/C A/C/H	305 A 312 B **350 B** **413 B** 277 293	2512 2315 **2317** 2219 3-60 4-39	XX75 XX75 **XX75** XX75,E A/C/C A/C/H	316 A 362 B **411 A** 427 B 287 303	2512 **2514** **2317** 3-71 4-49	XX75 **XX75** **XX75** A/C/C A/C/H	326 B **363 A** **424 B** 312 329	**2514** **2317** 2419 3-71 4-49	**XX75** **XX75** XX75 A/C/C A/C/H	**374 B** **438 C** 480 A 322 339
2512 2315 **2317** 2219 3-60 4-39	XX75 XX75 **XX75** XX75,E A/C/C A/C/H	305 A 350 B **398 A** 413 B 277 293	2512 **2514** **2317** 3-71 4-49	XX75 **XX75** **XX75** A/C/C A/C/H	316 B **351 A** **411 B** 302 318	**2514** **2317** 2419 3-71 4-49	**XX75** **XX75** XX75 A/C/C A/C/H	**363 B** **424 C** 466 A 312 329	2514 **2419** 3-71 4-49	XX75 **XX75** A/C/C A/C/H	374 B **480 A** 322 339
2512 **2514** **2317** 3-71 4-49	XX75 **XX75** **XX75** A/C/C A/C/H	305 B **340 A** **398 B** 293 308	**2514** **2317** 2419 3-71 4-49	**XX75** **XX75** XX75 A/C/C A/C/H	**351 B** **411 C** 451 A 302 318	2514 **2419** 3-71 4-49	XX75 **XX75** A/C/C A/C/H	363 B **466 A** 312 329	2419	XX75	480 A
2514 **2317** 2419 3-71 4-49	**XX75** **XX75** XX75 A/C/C A/C/H	**340 B** **398 C** 437 A 293 308	2514 **2419** 3-71 4-49	XX75 **XX75** A/C/C A/C/H	351 B **451 A** 302 318	2419	XX75	466 A			
2514 **2419** 3-71 4-49	XX75 **XX75** A/C/C A/C/H	340 B **437 A** 293 308	2419	XX75	451 A	If you use one of the following sizes: 2312, 2314, 2315, 2317, 2413, 2419, 2512, 2514 with an aluminum RPS insert, add the weight of that insert to your point weight, then subtract 25 grains and re-enter the point weight column within which this adjusted point weight falls.					

How to use the **EASTON SHAFT SELECTION CHARTS**

1. Determine your **Correct Arrow Length** and your **Actual, Actual Peak, Calculated** or **Calculated Peak Bow Weight**.
2. Under the column for recurve or compound bows, locate the box that includes your **Actual, Actual Peak, Calculated** or **Calculated Peak Bow Weight**.
3. Move across the row in a horizontal direction to the right until you locate the column including your **Correct Arrow Length**.
4. One or more recommended sizes are listed in the "Shaft Size" box located where your "**Actual, Actual Peak, Calculated** or **Calculated Peak Bow Weight**" row and "**Correct Arrow Length**" column intersect.

The "Variables" listed below will affect the **Actual Bow Weight** and **Actual Peak Bow Weight** as noted. Combine all the adjustments that apply to your equipment to figure your **Calculated Bow Weight** or **Calculated Peak Bow Weight**.

Variables to the "standard" set-up:

- High Energy Cam – add 10 lbs.
- Dacron String – subtract 3-5 lbs.
- Release Aids – subtract 3-5 lbs.
- Bow efficiency – subtract 3-5 lbs. for older less efficient bows
- Compound bow lengths 44" or less, and draw lengths over 28" – add 4-6 lbs.
- Point Weight – add 1.5 lbs. for every 10 grains your point weighs more than:
  -7% F.O.C. point, aluminum shaft
  -8% F.O.C. point, A/C/C or A/C/H shaft
  -recommended point weight, A/C/E shaft

Reading the **EASTON SHAFT SELECTION CHARTS**

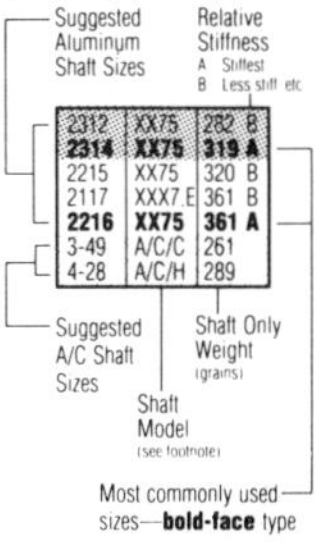

Suggested Aluminum Shaft Sizes
Relative Stiffness
A Stiffest
B Less stiff etc.
2312 XX75 282 B
2314 XX75 319 A
2215 XX75 320 B
2117 XXX7.E 361 B
2216 XX75 361 A
3-49 A/C/C 261
4-28 A/C/H 289
Suggested A/C Shaft Sizes
Shaft Only Weight (grains)
Shaft Model (see footnote)
Most commonly used sizes—bold-face type

C) Determining Arrow Length

Arrow length is, greatly influenced by the handle style of your bow. Overdraw arrow rests on handles with a center-shot tunnel allow the use of shorter arrows. Traditional handle risers with no center shot tunnel require hunting arrows that extend beyond the back of the bow. Shooting a *broadhead* from this style handle means the *arrow must extend beyond the handle riser by at least one-half inch* so the broadhead does not hit the handle or your fingers when the arrow is drawn to full draw. *Field point* equipped arrows need *extend only one-half inch beyond the arrow rest* with this style handle.

Handles with center shot tunnels and a standard rest location can accommodate broadhead equipped arrows that extend only one-half inch past the arrow rest. Tunnel handles with overdraw arrow rests also require arrows that extend at least one-half inch past the arrow rest. Allow that little extra length so you don't draw the arrow point or broadhead into the arrow rest or into your bow hand when the adrenalin is flowing.

When cutting aluminum or carbon shafts to length, always use a high speed cut-off tool with an abrasive wheel. Such a tool will not bend or distort the end of the shaft. A copper tube cut-off tool or a hacksaw can distort or bend the end of an arrow shaft. Be sure to remove any burr caused by the cutting process. Remember that arrow length is related to arrow spine. The shorter an arrow is cut, the stiffer it will act. Don't be too quick to cut your arrows short. A little test shooting before cutting to final length might change your mind about the length you need.

D) Fletch Selection

Once again, the number, length and type of fletching you need depends upon how you plan to use your arrows. Short range hunting shots and 20 yard target shooting can benefit from larger fletching so the arrow will stabilize quickly. Long range hunting shots and long range target shooting can benefit from short vanes which maintain speed, but that's only part of the picture for hunting shots. Increased speed can produce flatter trajectory, but accuracy is the ultimate goal, and there are many more elements than a fast arrow involved in accuracy. Most often, simply having the time to set up and take careful aim at an unalarmed animal can do more for accuracy than can any other factor. A fast miss is still a miss, and an arrow too light in mass to have good kinetic energy won't give the needed penetration. An arrow still flying somewhat sideways when it hits the target won't have the desired penetration either. Proper setup and tuning should prevent that problem.

Consistent grouping at the maximum distance you intend to shoot is the final determining factor in your choice of fletching. As a rough example, when you need quick stability large fletching (four or five inch vanes or feathers) will do that job well. On longer shots, maybe smaller broadheads and smaller fletching may work well to maintain arrow velocity and accuracy.

Long range target shooting requires small fletching and aerodynamic points. Target arrows with small, light weight points need only 1.75 inch or 2.00 inch fletching to achieve stable arrow flight. Small vanes are great for maintaining down range velocity and accuracy with target arrows, making good grouping at 90 and 100 yards possible. Small vanes lose less velocity but maintain stability since small aerodynamic arrow points are used. By the way, aerodynamic does not necessarily mean light weight, since some target points weigh as much as 125 grains.

E) Point Weight Selection

The weight of the arrow point controls the center of gravity of the arrow shaft. A shaft with no point has a center of gravity located very near the center of the shaft. A light point will move the center of gravity toward the point end of the shaft. Heavier points will move it even further toward the point.

The distance that the balance point lies in front of the center is referred to as F.O.C. (front of center) and is usually given as a percent of the total shaft length. Each size shaft requires a different weight point to create a 10% F.O.C. as shown in Fig. 88. **Each bow and arrow combination may require a different F.O.C. balance point to create the best groups possible.**

Literature supplied by A.F.C. and packaged with their carbon arrows contains a useful formula for calculating the percent F.O.C. for a given point weight. The formula involves the weight, in grains, of the various parts of the arrow, as well as their locations on the shaft.

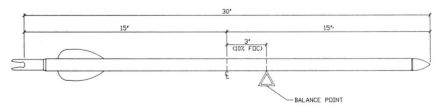

• *Fig. 88. For this 30 inch arrow, a 10% front of center balance point would be located three inches in front of the center of the shaft. For most shafts, this requires a point weighing between 100 and 125 grains.*

The formula is as follows:

VARIABLES:

A = total arrow length including point and nock
F = total weight of fletching
N = weight of nock
P = total point weight
R = F.O.C. percent in decimal form
W = shaft weight without nock, fletching or point
   (multiply grains per inch by length of shaft)

FORMULA 1: Calculating percent F.O.C. for a given point weight (P).

$$R = \left[\frac{.5 \times N + 2 \times F + .5 \times A \times W + (A-1) \times P}{N + F + W + P} - (.5 \times A) \right] \div A$$

Rearranging Formula 1 will give Formula 2, which calculates the point weight necessary to obtain a given percent F.O.C. balance. The values obtained will be accurate to within five grains of point weight.

FORMULA 2: Finding point weight for a given percent F.O.C.

$$P = \left[\frac{.5 \times N + 2 \times F - A \times (N+F) \times (.5+R) - R \times A \times W}{(R-.5) \times A + 1} \right]$$

Because a heavy point requires more energy to make it move, the arrow will bend more as thrust is applied to its lighter nock end. This means that heavy points make arrow shafts bend more and act weaker. Lighter points are easier to move, so a given arrow size will bend less when thrust is applied to the nock end. Lighter points make the arrow act stiffer.

Down range accuracy can be affected by small changes in spine caused by small changes in point weight. Twenty or 30 grains of point weight can be the only factor that is keeping your broadheads from grouping at 40 yards or your target arrows from grouping at 80 yards. Trying different point weights while group testing is the only way to find which percent F.O.C. balance point will yield the best groups for a given shaft size.

F) Common Fletching Procedures For Aluminum And Carbon Arrows

Carbon arrows are relatively new on the market and offer some advantages. The other side of the issue is that they require different techniques and procedures to build and tune. Those differences are highlighted in dark type in this chapter.

1) Shaft Preparation

Shaft preparation before fletching is an absolute must. Without a clean surface on the shaft, the glue you use may be totally ineffective. Nothing is more frustrating than getting to a tournament or to your hunting destination and having your fletching fall off.

Several simple steps can take care of this problem, depending upon the type of shaft you use. Aluminum shafts should be scrubbed with Ajax and warm water. Acetone can also be used. Rinse the shafts thoroughly with warm water and dry them with a paper towel. They are now ready for fletching, so do not handle the fletching area.

Carbon arrows should be cleaned with lacquer thinner or denatured alcohol. Acetone used on these shafts may leave residue that will attack the glue you use. An alternate method, which I recommend, is to sand the fletching area of the shaft with very fine sand paper and wipe clean with a dry cloth. This step must be given great attention so a good bond is established between the fletch and the shaft.

2) Nock Preparation

After the arrows are cleaned, twist the nocks snugly onto the end of the shaft. Do not use glue, because after the fletching is complete you will want to remove the nocks and rotate them to their proper position. This position is determined by powder testing — it shows whether the fletching is or is not hitting the arrow rest. When the best possible clearance is obtained with one shaft, glue all the nocks on the shafts in that position.

Carbon arrows require a little more preparation. The last half inch of both ends of a carbon shaft should be sanded with fine sand paper. This prepares the ends for receiving the nock adapter and the point. Wipe these ends with a dry cloth after sanding.

Clean both the nock adapter and the point with alcohol or acetone and glue them to the shaft. Be sure to glue the weight pin into the point before installing the point in the shaft. Use epoxy to insure the best bond. If you plan to use a hot melt glue, be sure to use one with a high melting temperature.

3) Fletch Preparation

Feathers do not usually require any cleaning or other preparation, but vanes do. Most vanes have a residue on them. This residue can destroy the bond between the vane and shaft if it is not removed.

Denatured alcohol is the best agent for cleaning vanes, although acetone can also be used. Place the vane in the glue clamp and wipe

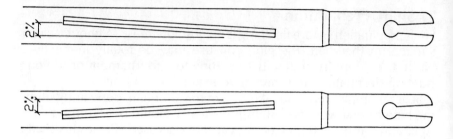

• *Fig. 89. Fletching should always be angled when placed on the shaft. Two or three degrees is normal for aluminum shafts, while one degree is sufficient for carbon shafts.*

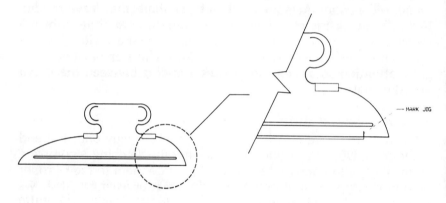

• *Fig. 90. The glue clamp should always be marked at the back edge of the fletch. All of the fletches will then be installed on the shaft the same distance from the nock.*

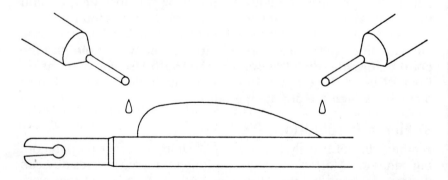

• *Fig. 91. A drop of glue placed on the ends of each fletch will give these vulnerable areas some added protection from damage when the arrow passes through targets and backstops.*

the base of the vane with a paper towel dipped in denatured alcohol. Clean all the vanes you intend to use and lay them aside, but do not touch the bases of the vanes.

4) Fletching

The actual fletching of the shaft begins with a test arrow and fletch. With the arrow in the jig and the fletch in the clamp, place the clamp on the jig next to the arrow. Adjust the angle of the clamp so both ends of the fletch will be sure to touch the arrow shaft. Do not place the fletchings in line with the shaft; they must be angled two or three degrees (Fig. 89).

Hunting vanes and feathers should be attached using a curved, helical clamp. The more angle used, the quicker the arrow will stabilize. Check the first fletch that you glue to see if it is angled correctly. Reset the glue clamp if it is not.

Carbon arrows, because of their small diameter and quick recovery, do not need as much offset on their fletching. Instead of two or three degrees, one degree offset should be enough. Hunting vanes and feathers should still be attached using a curved, helical clamp.

The type of glue you use for fletching carbon arrows is critical. Some glues do not bond well to carbon. Most instant glues like Super Instant Fletch Tite will bond well but leave little time for adjusting the fletch once it has touched the shaft. Non-instant glues, Saunders for example, will also work well on carbon. Be sure to test the fletching on the first shaft you do.

Before you begin fletching your arrows, mark the clamp where the back of the fletching is to be placed in it, as shown in Figure 90. This will insure that all of your fletches will be placed on the shaft the same distance from the nock.

Begin the fletching by placing a thin line of glue from one end of the fletch to the other. Don't leave any bare spots. This insures that glue will spread between all of the fletch and the shaft when the clamp is placed on the jig.

Next, push the clamp and fletch firmly against the shaft. If you are using a quick drying glue, then don't move it. If you use a non-instant glue, slide the clamp back and forth a little to insure that the glue is spreading evenly between the fletch and the shaft.

Instant cements should be left to dry three or four minutes. Other glues should be allowed to dry ten minutes.

Now, remove the clamp by first opening it and then pulling it away from the shaft. This will prevent pulling the fletch away from the shaft.

Following the fletching of an arrow, be sure to place a drop of glue on each end of each fletch. Gluing each end (Fig. 91) will keep the ends from being pulled away from the shaft when the arrow passes through a target. This extra step will give your fletching job longer life. Alow these drops and your fletching to dry for a day.

5) Point Installation

Once you have selected the point weight for your aluminum arrows, glue the points or inserts into the shaft. First heat the shank of the point or insert, then apply a small amount of hot-melt glue to the point. As you push the point into the shaft, rotate it so the glue spreads evenly around the point and inside of the shaft. Push the point against a board to insure that the point is all the way into the shaft. To prevent smearing the warm glue, allow the arrows to cool before you peel away excess glue on the outside of the shaft.

To remove the point and insert, simply reheat the point, not the shaft, until the point can be pulled from the shaft. Use pliers and a twisting motion for this job on aluminum arrows.

Epoxy glue should be used on the points of carbon arrows. Apply some to the weight pin and the end of the shaft. Push the point and pin straight into the shaft without twisting. Allow the glue to dry for half an hour before removing any excess on the outside of the point or shaft. When it is hard, the epoxy should peel away easily.

Removing the point and pin from a carbon arrow can be done by using low heat on the point but not on the shaft. Low heat will slowly break down the epoxy bond, and the point then can be pulled straight out of the shaft. Again, don't use a twisting motion.

6) Nock Installation

After the point is secure it is time to glue the nock in place. Remove the nock from the end of the shaft. After applying a drop of glue to the end of the shaft, place the nock on the end. Rotate the nock around the end several times so the glue spreads evenly between the nock and shaft.

Align the nock so fletch clearance is at its best. Spin the arrow in your hand to check the straightness of the nock. If it wobbles, realign it and test again until it is straight. Allow the adhesive to set for at least an hour to insure a good bond.

If you use an instant glue, be sure the nock is aligned the way you want it when you push it onto the shaft. You will have little time to rotate the nock after it touches the glued surface.

G) Tuning Aluminum Arrows

The procedure for tuning aluminum arrows is basically the same as the procedure for carbon arrows, which is detailed in the next section. The only difference is in the manner in which point weight is controlled. Carbon arrows have a brass weight pin that can be cut to any length or weight, while the aluminum arrow has only two or three different weight points.

To change the weight of aluminum arrow points, cut the shank of the target point shorter. Field points can be custom made to any weight if you know a machine shop which can do that kind of work.

Another alternative is to leave an extra inch or two on your aluminum shafts. During the group testing phase of tuning you can cut several arrows shorter by 1/4 inch or 1/2 inch increments and retest. After testing different lengths until the arrow is as short as you can shoot it accurately, you should be able to determine the best grouping spine or length.

Keep these ideas in mind while you read the next section on the carbon arrow.

H) Tuning The Carbon Arrow
1) Introduction

Even though carbon arrows are new, proper established tuning procedures still apply. Tuning carbon arrows, like tuning aluminum arrows, involves the following techniques and rules:

a) Final shaft selection done by shoot testing.

b) Nocking point checked by bare shaft testing or by paper testing.

c) Slightly stiff shafts for your bow will shoot better than slightly weak shafts.

d) Longer shaft lengths will act weaker than shorter shafts of the same diameter.

e) Heavier point weights will make a given shaft act weaker, while lighter weight points allow the shaft to act stiffer.

f) Contact between fletches and arrow rest should be avoided.

g) You may encounter glue problems with some vanes on carbon.

2) How The Carbon Arrow Is Different

Carbon shafts are new and different. The main differences are as follows:

a) Smaller diameters.

b) Higher stiffness to weight ratio.

c) Faster arrow speed.

d) Quicker arrow stabilization.

e) Deeper penetration.

f) Different arrow rest requirements.

g) Center shot adjustment of rest requires the cushion plunger or the side plate to be slightly further from sight window of the bow.

h) Fletch angle can be reduced slightly.

i) Nocking point will be slightly lower.

j) Carbon requires different care, certain vanes and adhesives.

3) Tuning Procedure

Select the size shaft indicated as proper for your draw weight and arrow length. Use the AFC comparison chart for carbon versus aluminum and also the Peak Weight versus Arrow Length chart. This is not an exact science for any shaft and is intended to obtain several shafts that will shoot well. Individual bow and shooter characteristics may require a change of one or two shaft sizes to get optimum results. When in doubt, choose the slightly stiffer shaft size.

Cut the carbon shafts one inch longer than the aluminum arrows you have been using. The extra length will help compensate for the greater stiffness of the carbon shaft and allow experimenting by removing 1/4 inch segments to observe spine and grouping changes.

Your arrow rest must be altered so it will support the smaller carbon arrow while allowing fletch clearance. The side plate or cushion plunger will need to be further from the side of the bow since the carbon arrows are smaller in diameter. Check the clearance with white powder foot spray. No vane or feather should be contacting the rest. A launcher style rest with a narrow point launcher should work well for release shooters. Finger shooters should try an A.T. Olympiad or a Cavalier T300 with a Flipper II or similar rest combinations.

The nocking point location for carbon arrows will be about 1/16 to 1/8 inch lower than for the larger aluminum arrows. Start tuning with a setting of about 1/8 to 3/16 inch above level. This should allow the bottom of the shaft to be level.

The brass or stainless steel weight pin used in the arrow points can be cut to obtain an F.O.C. (front of center) balance point of 7% to 11%. Measure the arrow length from the bottom of the nock throat to the tip of the point. Calculate 7% to 11% of the length and mark your arrows that far in front of the center of the shaft. Cut the balance pin to obtain the desired balance point.

You may want to start tuning with two fletched and two non-fletched arrows and a full length weight pin. Bare shaft test or group test as you cut the balance pin shorter. This would assure finding the balance point which produces best grouping.

Target arrows should be fletched using 1.75 inch or 2.00 inch straight vanes placed on the shaft with a one degree offset. You can also try 1.75 inch or 2.9 inch spin-wing vanes.

Hunting arrow preparation would require using the brass balance pin or the heavier stainless steel balance pin. The total pin and point weight should be approximately the same as the broadhead you intend to use. Four-inch vanes or feathers should provide adequate stabilization for most broadheads on carbon arrows. You can reduce the angle of helical curve used since the carbon tends to recover quicker than aluminum.

Most finger shooters begin bare shaft testing at approximately 15 feet and continue out to 30 feet. Adjust your nocking point so the bare shaft is entering at about the same height as a fletched shaft. Adjust the point and pin weight so bare shafts enter nock left (for right handed shooter) with heavy points but tend to enter straighter as point weight is reduced. Group test from long range with each point weight. Shaft length can also be altered to gain the desired bare shaft result.

Most release shooters begin paper testing at about 10 feet and continue to about 30 feet. The nocking point should be set so the nock end of the arrow is tearing a near perfect hole or testing straight high or high left (for right handed shooter) no more than 3/4 inch.

Begin with the full length weight pin that gives an 11% F.O.C. balance, using at least three arrows. Paper test as you reduce point weight by cutting 1/4 inch sections from the pin. Also group test from long range as point weight is reduced. By the time you have cut your three experimental arrows as short as you dare shoot safely, you should know what point weight groups the best.

Broadhead testing begins with field points about the same weight as the broadhead you intend to use. Use the paper testing procedure. You may try altering point weight if you are not locked into using a given weight broadhead. To get good results, you may have to change to a different point weight or to a different shaft spine. At this point, you should employ the tuning steps mentioned in an earlier chapter.

JON
WERT
87

Building and Tuning Arrows

Chapter 12

What Must A Broadhead Be, What Must It Do?

by Sherwood Schoch, with Norb Mullaney

Bow tuning is critical to the tournament archer, but it is even more critical to the bowhunter. Tournament shooters need only to strike a mark to have a perfect scoring arrow; it really doesn't matter how far the target arrow penetrates. **It is very important to the bowhunter how far the arrow penetrates.**

Our primary goal as bowhunters is to achieve complete arrow penetration — two holes in the quarry. That generally will assure the best and earliest blood trail. Regarding our equipment, attaining that goal is dependent upon the following:

• Any good broadhead can be made better by being made sharper.

• When the arrow's fletching rotates the arrow it greatly assists in the stabilization of that arrow, because it counteracts the attempt of the broadhead to take over control of the flight.

• The fletching system must be designed so that it will always assume positive control of the arrow, overcoming any tendency of the broadhead to take over control of the flight path.

Where launching and tuning comes in is that you must tune the bow and arrow combination so that it launches the arrow in such a manner that it is properly directed when it leaves the bow. The arrow must be flying right until the fletching takes over and controls the arrow on its path to the target.

• The best penetration possible with a given bow and arrow combination is when the arrow is tuned exactly correct to the bow.

• Properly tuned arrows will fly truer to the intended mark.

• If the arrow is flying straight and true, without yaw or pitch, it makes maximum use of the energy it has and does not dissipate any of the energy needlessly, which will allow best possible penetration. The less an arrow is wiggling and wobbling when it gets to the target, the more of its energy is used for penetration since the maximum energy is directed in line with the shaft . . . and the better penetration will be. Consequently, you should strive to get the very best flying arrow possible if you want the best opportunity to retrieve every animal you hit.

What we as bowhunters and shooters must achieve is a tune match of the arrow to the bow so the arrow flies as soon as possible and as closely as possible on perfect column, thus minimizing the rudder effect of the blades on the front end. ("Perfect column" means that the flight path of the arrow is in line with its longitudinal axis.)

Have you ever launched a broadhead-tipped arrow, watched it fly very well for 15 or 20 yards, then suddenly veer off in some direction? This is what happens when the broadhead overrides the control of the fletching. When the front end takes over the steering, the arrow begins to veer off course.

The broadhead's grain weight and the location of the center of that weight are important in determining how the arrow will fly out of a given bow/arrow/draw-weight and tuning combination. Generally speaking, the heavier the broadhead and the further that center of weight is positioned forward, the stiffer the arrow must be so as not to flex too much as it leaves the bow. A short broadhead may weigh the same as a longer one, but its center of gravity may be further aft, causing the dynamic stiffness of the arrow to be greater.

The same effect takes place when we compare broadheads and field points of equal weight. The center of gravity of the broadhead is most likely further forward of the center of gravity of the field point, and when this is the case it will make the arrow less dynamically stiff.

It is important that the broadhead be exactly aligned with the shaft. If the broadhead is slightly angled or not on true center line, it almost always has an adverse effect upon the arrow's flight. If the broadhead is slightly bent or leaning in any direction off the shaft's true center line, the blades will have an angle of attack relative to the flight path of the arrow and will tend to steer the arrow off that flight path, thus creating less accuracy and poorer penetration.

The penetration will be adversely affected in several ways by the misaligned broadhead. First, the arrow will not fly as accurately during its flight. Second, the broadhead will have a greater effect on the steering of the arrow. Third, when the arrow reaches the intended quarry, because of the non-perfect alignment of the broadhead to the shaft, the broadhead will tend to push sideways as well as ahead as it tries to penetrate. This action will dissipate some of the energy of the arrow that should be used for penetration.

In most cases there is an easy test to determine broadhead alignment, and it works best for broadheads with ferrules and replaceable blades. If you spin the arrow on its point, and it does not wobble, chances are it is properly aligned. However, for broadheads where the tip of the blade is the leading point, this test is not always adequate. If the point is ground "off", so the tip is not in line with the exact center line of the broadhead, the arrow will wobble when spun, even though the blades and ferrule are perfectly in line.

The most positive way to check blade alignment on all broadhead types is with V blocks and dial indicator gauge which can be used to transverse the blades.

The type and size of the fletching, and the angle (to the center line) at which it is attached to the shaft, will determine how much control is offered by the fletched end of the shaft. An arrow that has helical or offset fletching, five inches long, will be more controlled than a shaft with straight five-inch fletching attached in line with the shaft. Feather fletching has more drag and hence offers more control than vane fletching of the same size and orientation.

It is necessary to have a fletching system that is adequate to control the broadhead being used. However, it is important to remember that the more control drag that is provided by the fletching system, the greater is the down range velocity loss. Full contour (normally 9/16-inch to 5/8-inch high), five inches long, three-fletch, helical feather or vane fletching will handle most broadheads. An equivalent full contour, four-inch, four-fletch arrangement will do the same job. For very large broadheads, it may be necessary to use larger fletching.

Many times a question arises as to whether the fletching should be right or left angled. If the broadhead blades are in line with the center line of the shaft, once the arrow is in flight, having cleared the bow, it really doesn't make any difference. However, the design of the arrow rest, the degree of center shot of the bow, and the type of fletching all may dictate that either right or left hand fletching will provide better fletching clearance as the arrow leaves the bow. This is something which must be determined based on the individual setup.

Recently, we have seen broadheads where the blades are angled to increase the rotation action of the arrow. In this case, the fletching and the broadhead blades must have their angles aligned both right or both left, and even better if they are at the same angle.

The more blades on a broadhead, the more drag exists upon penetration, but the more blood vessels it will cut. Penetration is not the only answer; the number of blood vessels cut is also very important.

Much has been written about the number of blades most desirable on broadheads. Typical of many things in archery, this is not a clear-cut, black and white decision. There are pros and cons.

It is generally conceded that all things being equal — two-bladed heads will penetrate deeper than multi-bladed heads, and depth of penetration is a critical thing. On the other hand, multi-bladed heads cut more flesh and blood vessels, and open larger holes. This is an important factor, too.

In addition, multi-bladed heads generally are easier to control in flight because they usually have lower profile blades, and the head is less susceptible to planing (because of the lower profile and better aerodynamic balance). As an extreme comparison, throw a stick and a wood shingle into the wind and compare how they fly.

With compound bows which have exposed cables, we must be as certain that the fletching does not contact the cables as it leaves the bow. It will adversely affect the flight of the arrow if the fletching strikes the cables on the way past.

Bowhunters used the archer's paradox to their advantage for hundreds of years. Today, archer's paradox is greatly minimized, with bows generally more centershot, particularly with compound bows. The use of a release aid, as contrasted to finger shooting, also reduces paradox. It reduces or eliminates the swing to the side which occurs as the string comes off the fingers.

This greatly reduces the flexing in the shaft as it comes out of the bow, promoting true in-line flight much sooner. Because of this, the use of a release aid permits wider tolerance in shaft selection since the exact stiffness of the shaft becomes less critical.

If you are not shooting your bow on true center line, then the arrow will take on a greater amount of flex as the energy is transferred from the bow to the arrow. When an arrow flexes, the magnitude of the oscillations depend upon the spine of the shaft, the weight of the head and fletching, the location of these weights on the shaft, and the amount of energy being applied to it. The greater the energy being applied to the rear end of the arrow, the stiffer the shaft must be; the greater the weight of the broadhead and fletching, the stiffer the shaft must be to minimize flexing. It is ill-advised to use heavy points on weak spined arrows. Generally speaking, as the arrow shaft spine is reduced, the grain weight of the point should be reduced.

In recent years, the over-draw arrow rest has become popular with some bowhunters using compound bows. The main reason is that you can get high velocity by shooting a lighter weight arrow than ordinarily would be used for the same draw-length, draw-weight bow. As a given arrow is cut shorter, its dynamic spine or stiffness increases. An arrow that is cut four inches shorter than normal might be used through a bow that is 20 pounds heavier in draw weight. By example, an arrow that is 30 inches long and matched to a 60-pound bow would become a match for an 80-pound bow if four inches were cut off, making the arrow 26 inches long. The shorter shaft does not flex as much, consequently, with the tuning right, you will or should get truer flight. However, because of its shorter length it may be less stable in flight.

The lower weight arrow has less kinetic energy, which can result in less penetration. The lighter arrow has the advantage of higher velocity and flatter trajectory, and this can be an important factor in the plus/minus error you can make in range estimation.

Another factor: In many instances, when less spine is required, the diameter of the shaft can be reduced. **Reducing the diameter can result in better penetration because the shaft will have less drag while it is penetrating and thus penetrate deeper.** In essence, a smaller diameter shaft of the same weight and velocity will penetrate better than a large diameter shaft.

The new graphite shafts have the potential for greater penetration because of their smaller diameter for a given spine.

Many broadhead blades are vented to provide less projected area. Since the rudder effect is related to the projected area, the rudder effect is therefore reduced. This makes the broadhead easier to control in flight, as compared to a solid blade of the same area.

It must be noted, as well, that the height of the blade or its actual distance off center line will have a compounded effect on the ease with which the arrow can be controlled in flight. The wider the blade on the shaft, the more leverage that blade has to control the rotation and direction of the arrow in flight.

The low profile broadhead has become popular with the over-draw shooting system, primarily for the following reasons: 1) Often a low profile head is required to clear the sight window; 2) the low profile head usually is lighter in weight and better matches the lighter weight arrow. In addition, shorter arrows are less stable, and the low profile head makes them easier to control. The smaller sized broadhead or lower profile broadhead will have less adverse effect upon the arrow flight and less resistance upon contact with the animal.

Many states have a regulation as to minimum cutting width of a broadhead. We must always stay within the bounds of the bowhunting laws, but we should always strive to shoot a broadhead that provides best flight and best penetration with good cutting action.

Here's a base-point rule of thumb: A 300-grain fletched shaft matched with a 120-grain broadhead is a good weight proportion for a draw weight which is properly matched to that total grain weight and spine. If the grain weight of the point (for this particular setup) is more than that, it is highly probable the broadhead will begin to steer this arrow early in its flight.

The size broadhead you choose should be the size which provides best arrow flight and maximum penetration for your bow setup. Remember, the object is to shoot entirely through the animal.

The optimum bow-arrow broadhead match for you is attainable and available with research and fine tuning. The best penetration possible comes along with this good tuning. Only the best tuned bow/arrow combination will provide you with the maximum benefit during the moment of truth.

• . . . and always remember to check the wind.

What Must a Broadhead Be and Do?

• As with all efforts regarding bow tuning, bow shooting and bowhunting, Murphy's Law is inescapable. Momma said there would be days like that. So you accept them and go on.

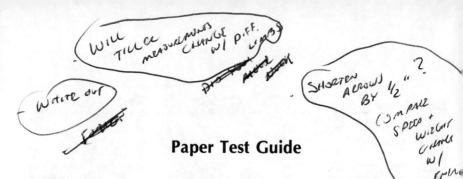

Paper Test Guide

Instructions

When the nock end of the arrow tears in any of the eight directions shown, then make a combination of the indicated adjustments.

Right Hand Shooter
(left hand shooter must reverse left/right adjustments)

Lower Nocking Point
Weaken Launcher

Lower Nock Point		Lower Nocking Point
Weaken Launcher		Weaken Launcher
Stiffen Side Tension		Weaken Side Tension
Less Draw Weight		More Draw Weight

Stiffen Side Tension	@	Weaken Side Tension
Less Draw Weight		More Draw Weight

Raise Nock Point		Raise Nocking Point
Stiffen Side Tension		More Draw Weight
Less Draw Weight		Weaken Side Tension
Stiffen Launcher		Stiffen Launcher

Raise Nocking Point
Stiffen Launcher

132

BOW FACT SHEET

Owner: BILL MOORE

Manufacturer: CLEARWATER ARCHERY

Model: X-TRA LITE Serial Number: O-0093-86-40

Recurve: N/A Longbow: N/A Compound: ✓

Two-Wheel: N/A Four-Wheel: N/A Two-Cam: ✓

Riser Material: Wood N/A Magnesium ______ Aluminum ______

True Draw Length: With finger tab: N/A

With release aid ______

Traditional Draw Length: With finger tab: N/A

With release aid ______

Peak Weight at Your Draw Length ______

Compound Bow Holding Weight in the Valley ______

Pounds of Let-Off (peak wt. hold wt.): 19

Percent Let-Off (pounds of let-off / peak wt.) ______ [illegible]

Tiller Measurements: Top Limb: [illegible] 9 5/16 [illegible] 9 1/8 9 3/16 [illegible]

Bottom Limb: [illegible] 9 5/16 [illegible] 9 1/8 9 3/16 [illegible]

Static Tip Deflection (pre-bend): Top Limb ______

Bottom Limb ______

Brace Height: [illegible] Nocking Point Height: 0°

String Length: 57 3/4 Number of Strands: 18

Distance of Peep Above Nocking Point: 4 7/16 ~~FROM TOP OF NOCK PT~~

Limb Type: Wood N/A Laminated Fiberglass: CARBON GLASS

Laminated Fiberglass w/ Wood Core ______

Fiber Reinforced Plastic: ✓

ARROW WIEGHT ~~490~~ GR. 498 27"

ARROWS 2215

ON ANNUAL BASIS: CHANGE CAM BUSHINGS, LUBE + TUNE

Tuning Fact Sheet

Date _____

Bow Brand _CLEARWATER_ _____ Model _XTRA LYTE_ _____

Peak Weight _____ Hold Weight _____

Arrow Size _____ Arrow Length _____

Field Point Weight __185__ _____

Broadhead: Weight __125__ _____

Number of Blades __3__ _____

~~Blade~~ Angle: Straight _____ Left _____ Right _____

Nock Size _____ Number of Strands in Bowstring _____

Fletching Type: Feathers _____ Vanes __✓_____

Number of Fletches __3_____ Length of Fletches __5"_____

Angle of Installation: Right _____ Straight _____ Left _____

Right Helical _____ Left Helical _____

Arrow Rest: Brand _TIGER TUFF TUFFY HUNTER W/O LONGHORN CUR LAUNCHER_

Type: Shoot-Around __N/A_____ Shoot-Through __✓_____

Mount Position: Standard _____ Overdraw _____

Nock Fit: Good _____ Tight _____ Loose _____

Initial Nocking Point Location __0°_____

Note: Nocking point location is the distance above a line which extends at a 90-degree angle from the bowstring and lies on the arrow rest. This location is measured to the **bottom** of the nocking point locator, with the arrow nocked **below** the nocking point locator. Thus, the nocking point height also can be defined as the distance to the top side of the arrow nock as it is nocked in the position defined here.

Field Point Testing

Powder Test: Contact _____ No Contact _____

Adjustments _____

_____

	(High)	(Left)
Paper Test: Nock End is Tearing	(Level) and	(Center)
	(Low)	(Right)

Adjustments _____

_____

~~15 YARDS: Arrows in Gold~~ = _____ ~~(Goal = 6 of 9)~~

~~Others~~ = _____

~~25 YARDS: Arrows in Gold/Red~~ = _____ ~~(Goal = 6 of 9)~~

~~Others~~ = _____

~~45 YARDS: Arrows in Gold/Red/Blue~~ = _____ ~~(Goal = 6 of 9)~~

~~Others~~ = _____ *(BOTTOM OF NOCK SET)*

Adjustments: Nocking Point _0-0 FROM TOP ARM OF REST_

Centershot _INSIDE OF B/D to CENTER OF ARROW 5/8'_

Rest Tension _____

Arrow Size _2215 GAME GETTER II ~~27~~"_

Draw Weight _~~70#~~ ~~65#~~ 60# (JUST A HAIR UNDER)_

Draw Length _62# 26 1/4" to FRONT ARM ON REST_

Others _KISSER BUTTON: ~~1 3/4~~ 1 11/16 UP FROM_

CENTER OF NOCK

PEEP SIGHT: ~~5 1/4~~ 5 5/16" UP FROM CENTER OF NOCK TO MIDDLE OF PEEP

Broadhead Testing

Straightness Check: Ferrules are Straight with Shaft _____

Arrows are Straight _____

Powder Test: Contact _____ No Contact _____

Adjustments _____

Paper Test: Nock end is tearing (High)　　(Left)
(optional)　　　　　　　　　　　　(Level) and (Center)
　　　　　　　　　　　　　　　　 (Low)　　(Right)

Adjustments _____

_____

15 YARDS: Arrows in Gold = _____ (Goal = 6 of 9)

Others _____ = _____

Adjustments_____

_____

25 YARDS: Arrows in Gold/Red = _____ (Goal = 6 of 9)

Others _____ = _____

Adjustments_____

_____

35 YARDS: Arrows in Gold/Red/Blue = _____ (Goal = 6 of 9)

Others _____ = _____

Adjustments_____

_____

45 YARDS: Arrows in Gold/Red/ = _____ (Goal = 6 of 9)
　　　　　　　　　　Blue/Black

Others _____ = _____

Adjustments_____

_____

58.51

55 YARDS: Arrows in Gold/Red/Blue/ = _____ (Goal = 6 of 9)
                    Black/White
       Others _____ = _____

       Adjustments _____

            _____

65 YARDS: Arrows in Gold/Red/Blue/ = _____ (Goal = 6 of 9)
                    Black/White
       Others _____ = _____

       Adjustments _____

            _____

Adjustment: Nocking Point _____

            Centershot _____

            Rest Tension _____

            Arrow Size _____

            Draw Weight _____

            Draw Length _____

            Others _____

                   _____

                   _____

KINETIC ENERGY FORMULA

$$FPS^2 \times ARROW\ WEIGHT$$

$$\div \quad \text{5851 ft lbs}$$

450240

POSSIBLY SHORTEN DRAW LENGTH 1/4"

The "On Target" Series

UNDERSTANDING WINNING ARCHERY, by Al Henderson, coach of the 1976 U.S. Olympic Archery Team, international coach and shooting consultant. Mental control means winning archery, easier archery gear set-up and practice. Book #01-001; $9.95 plus shipping/handling.

SUCCESSFUL TURKEY HUNTING, by J. Wayne Fears, wildlife biologist, turkey hunter and guide, calling contest judge. Book #01-002; $9.95 plus shipping/handling.

TAKING TROPHY WHITETAILS (2nd Edition), by Bob Fratzke with Glenn Helgeland. In-depth, detailed information on year-round scouting, scrape hunting, rut hunting, late season hunting, camo, use of scents plus entire new chapter on mock scraping and licking branches. Book #01-003; $9.95 plus shipping/handling.

SUCCESSFUL BOWFISHING, by Glenn Helgeland. A coast-to-coast, in-depth view of an enjoyable extension of your bowhunting. Freshwater and saltwater, carp to sharks, plus gear set-up, boat and canoe rigging, light diffraction and more. Book #01-004; $9.95 plus shipping/handling.

TO HELL WITH GRAVY wild game cookbook, by Glenn and Judy Helgeland. Gourmet results from quick, easy recipes. Includes 209 recipes plus meat handling/processing tips, spice chart, low-sodium diet tips and more. Book #01-005; $12.95 plus shipping/handling.

TASTY JERKY RECIPES FOR EVERYONE, by Glenn and Judy Helgeland. Spicy, mild, sweet and no-sodium recipes for three different meat cut thicknesses and tenderness. Make in oven, smoker, dehydrator or microwave. Book #01-006; $2.50 plus stamped, addressed #10 return envelope.

BATTLING BUCKS, by Noel Feather with Glenn Helgeland. Feather is the premier antler rattler in the country, having taken three Boone & Crockett trophies rattling. Scouting, set-up, use of scents and rattling, and more. Book #01-007; $14.95 plus shipping/handling.

TUNING YOUR COMPOUND BOW (2nd Edition), by Larry Wise, the recognized master at understanding and interpreting the mechanics of compound bows. Includes pre-use bow preparation, draw stroke, power stroke, shooting from the valley, fine tuning, test shooting, plus tuning the Fast Flite cable system, building and tuning aluminum and carbon arrows. Book #01-008; $10.95 plus shipping/handling.

TUNING YOUR BROADHEADS (2nd Edition), by Larry Wise. Problem-solving information on fitting the bow to your body and shooting form; broadhead effects on arrow flight; noise reduction; aiming and shooting strategies; proper practice; plus tuning the Fast Flite cable system, building and tuning aluminum and carbon arrows. Book #01-009; $10.95 plus shipping/handling.

SHIPPING & HANDLING		All prices (books and s/h) are in U.S. funds.
$10.00 or less	$2.00	
$10.01 - $20.00	$2.50	
$20.01 - $30.00	$3.00	
$30.01 - $60.00	$4.00	See your dealer or order direct
$60.01 - $100.00	$4.50	from the publisher (MC/VISA accepted).
Over $100.00	$4.95	

Write or call for a free catalog:

TARGET COMMUNICATIONS CORPORATION
7626 W. Donges Bay Rd.
Mequon, WI 53092
414/242-3990